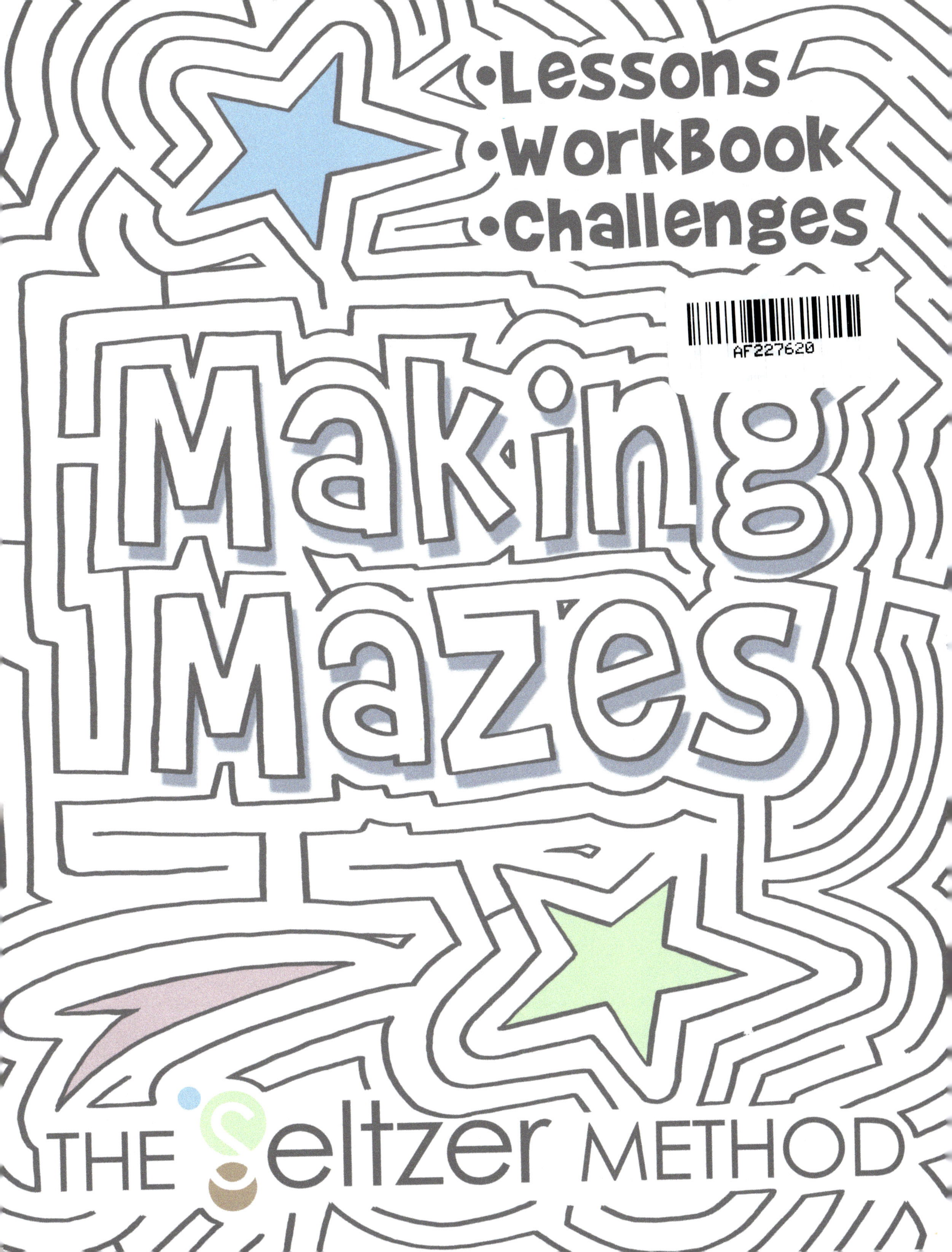

•Lessons
•WorkBook
•Challenges
AF227620
Making Mazes
THE Seltzer METHOD

Written and illustrated by Jerry Joe Seltzer

For more information visit TheSeltzerMethod.com

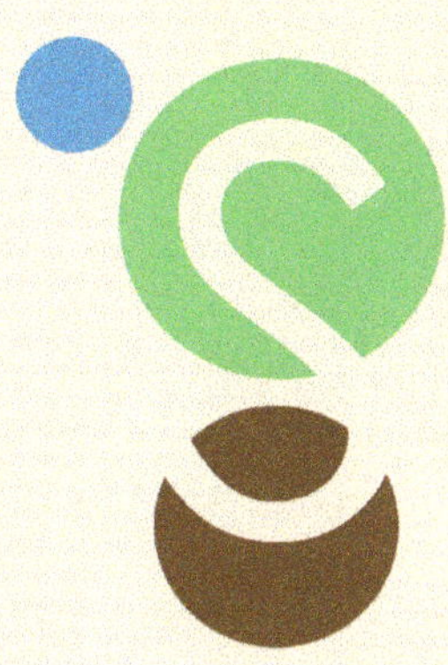

# Table of Contents

# How to build a maze using The Seltzer Method.

You will need a pencil. You will also need an eraser and a fine tip marker or pen. On the right-hand page, begin by drawing a circle roughly the size of a quarter. It doesn't need to be a good circle. It's fine if it looks like a potato. This shape is the <u>seed</u> of the maze. The rest of the maze will grow from this seed.

The next step is to draw a ring around the seed shape. This will create a pathway in between the lines. The pathway should be about 1 centimeter wide. If you aren't sure how big a centimeter is, it is roughly the same as the width of your pencil.

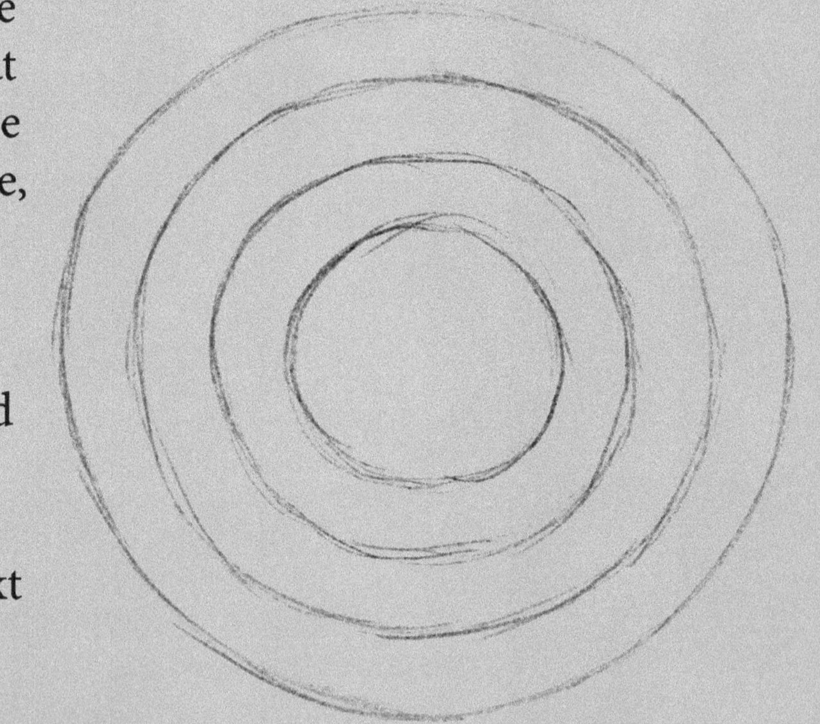


In all the mazes we create, we will try to keep all the pathways 1 cm wide. When a pathway becomes too narrow, the participant can't be sure if they are allowed to pass that way or not. So, we want to keep the paths wide, but if they are too wide, then we will quickly run out of room for our maze.

Draw a few more pathways around your maze. You should end up with something that looks like a bullseye. Turn the page for the next steps.



**Making Mazes** LESSONS, CHALLENGES, & WORKBOOK

Next, in each of your pathways, you will put up walls. Put two or three walls up in each. You are dividing each path into sections that we will need for our maze.

For this maze, we will be trying to get to the center. Write the word END in the center. Then pick a spot outside your maze and label that START.

Now it is time for your eraser. Erase a doorway through the wall by your START. Then, slowly knock open more doorways in the walls, making your way through the whole maze.

The goal is to use every section of every pathway even if it is only a dead end. Try weaving in and out of rings to fake out the person trying to solve it.

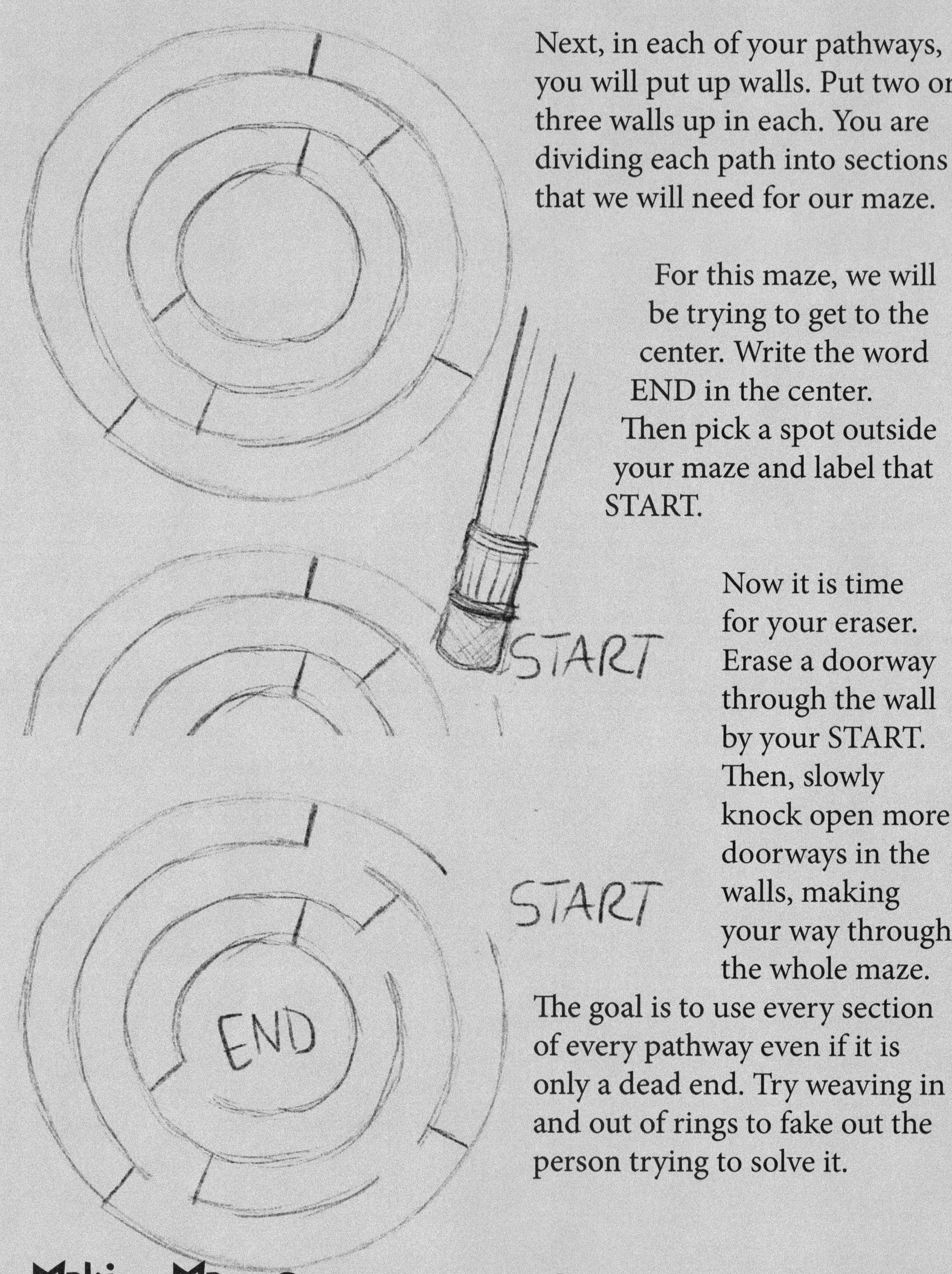




# Making Mazes LESSONS, CHALLENGES, & WORKBOOK

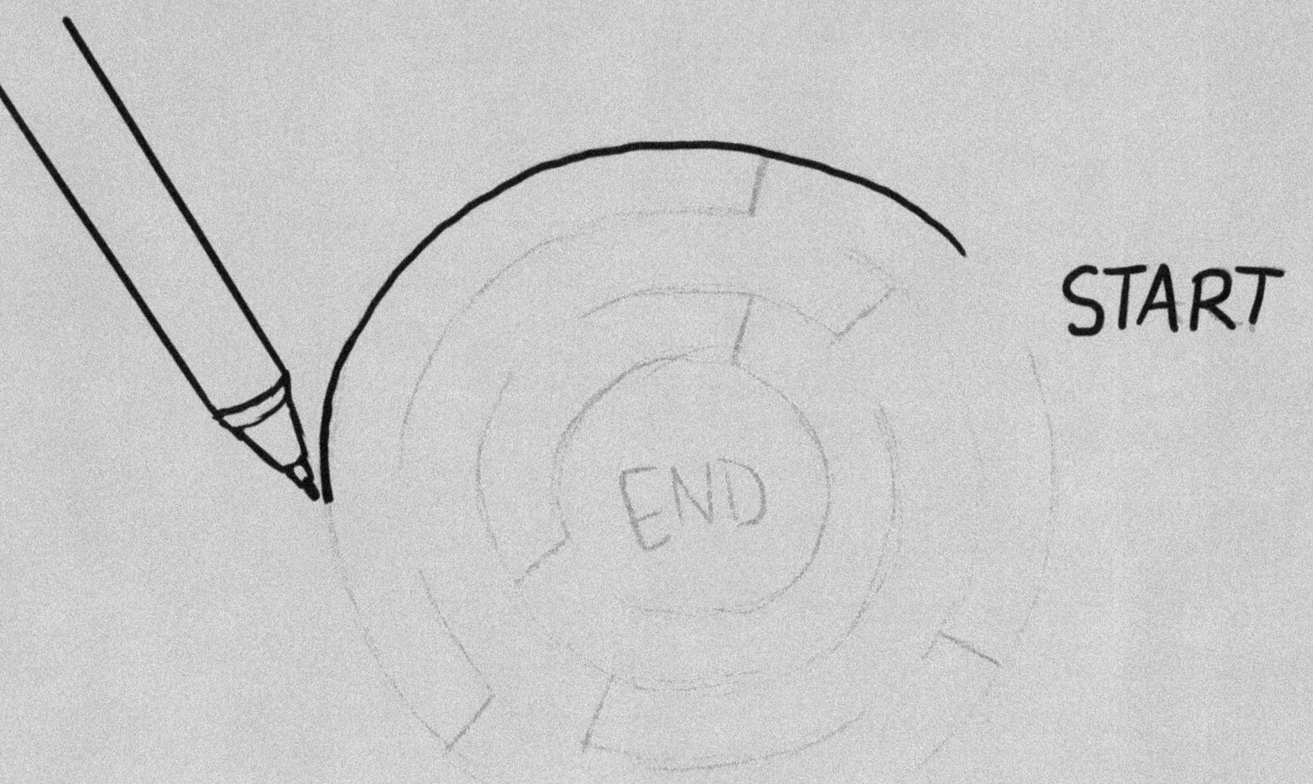


Finally, it is time to break out that marker. The Sharpie fine point marker works great for this. You will trace your pencil lines using the marker. This is called inking. As you do this, be very careful of the doorways you erased. It is very easy to draw right over them, closing them up for good.

Once you have finishing inking, and the ink has dried, you can use your eraser to clean up any visible pencil lines.

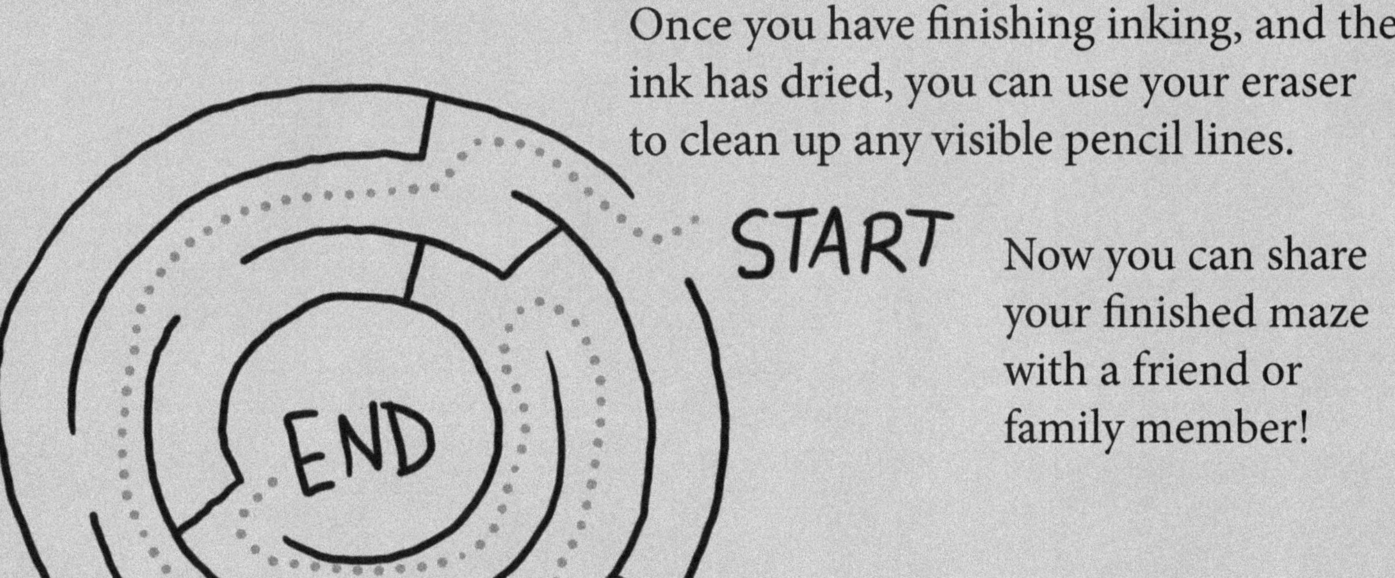


Now you can share your finished maze with a friend or family member!

# Using two shapes to build a maze.

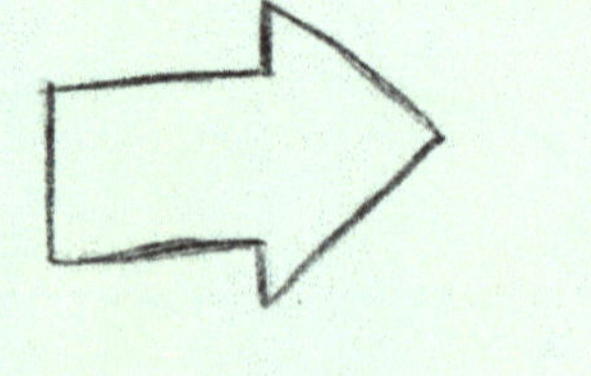
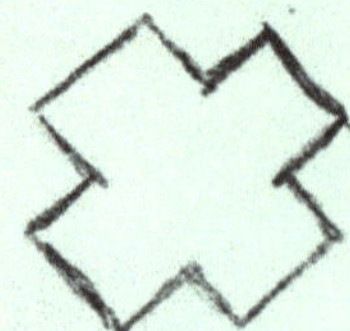

In the previous example you learned to make a maze using a small circle. That circle was the seed of the maze. In this exercise, you will use two seeds.

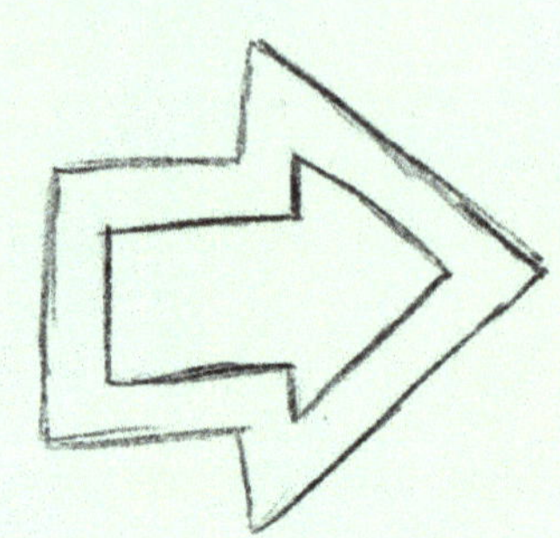
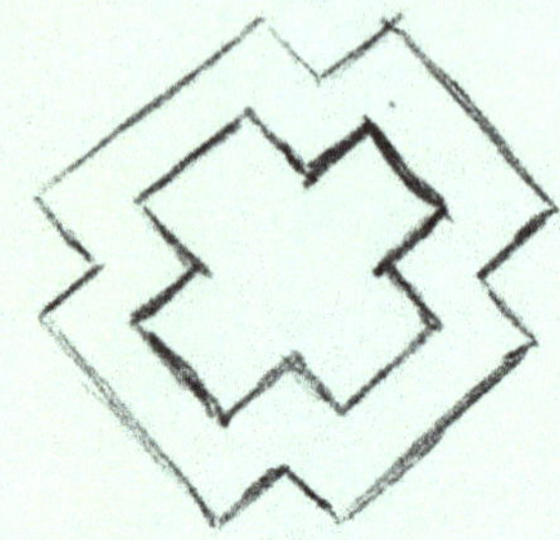

We start with two shapes, in this case an arrow and an x. Draw a pathway around each. You'll notice that as you add pathways, the areas begin growing closer to each other.

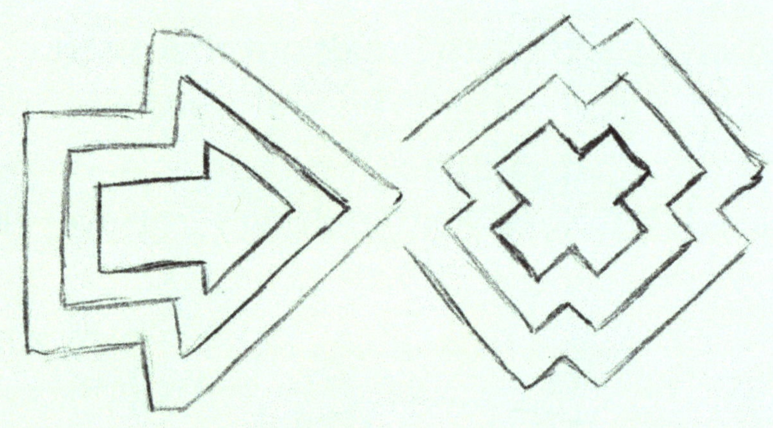

Once the two sections of maze are close enough, you will treat them like one big shape. The next pathway will go all the way around both shapes.

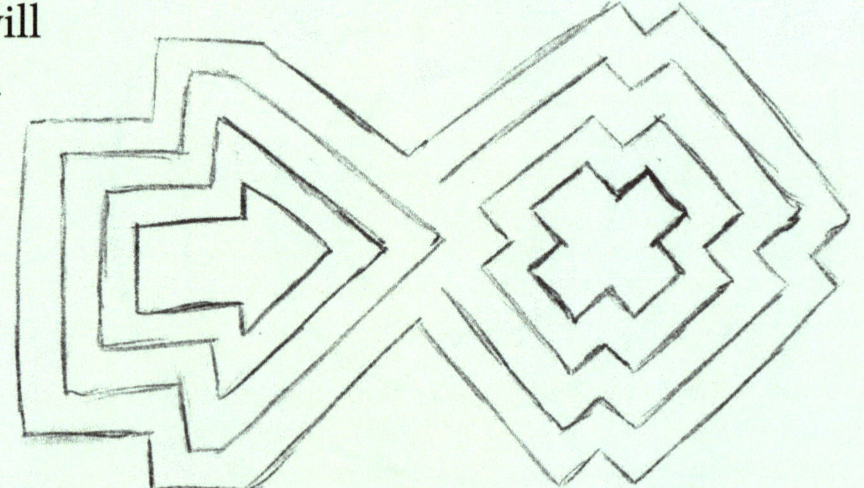



**Making Mazes** LESSONS, CHALLENGES, & WORKBOOK

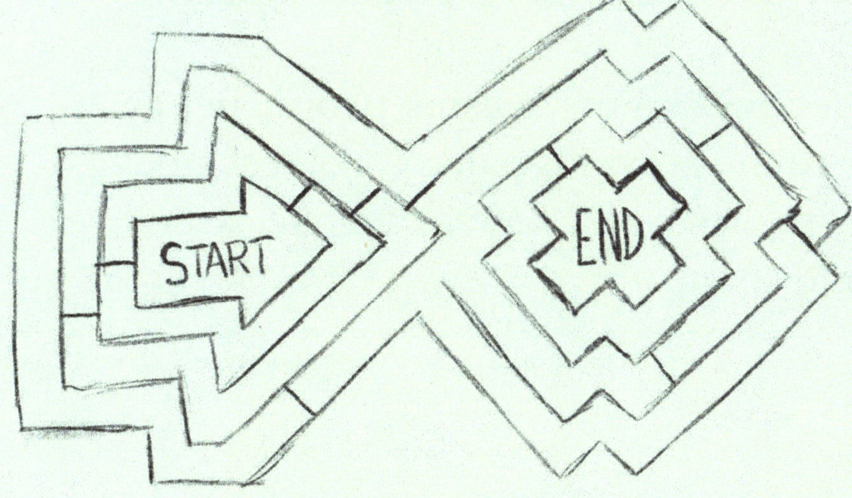


When you are done adding pathways, choose which shape will be the START and which will be the END.

 Put up walls in the pathways, dividing each one into sections

Then it is time to use your eraser. Begin making doorways by erasing holes in the walls. Try to make use of all the pathway sections. Erase your way from START to END.

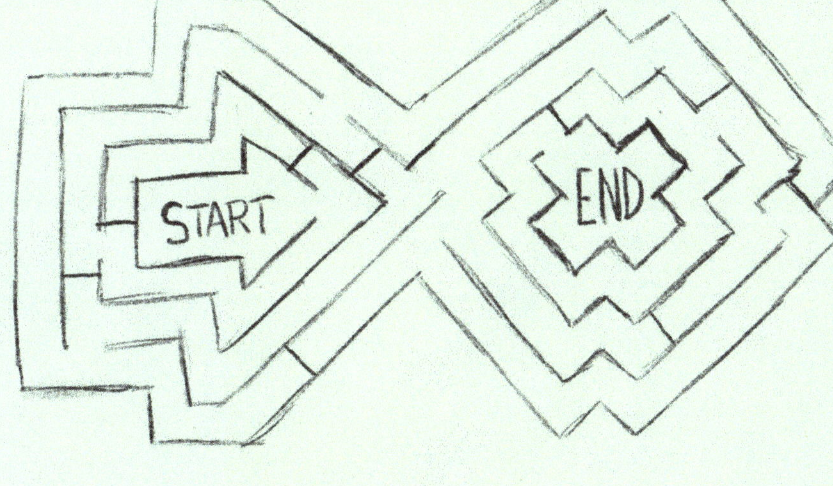


 Before you get your marker out and ink the lines, check your work. Can the maze be solved? Is it too easy? If so, you can add walls to eliminated shortcuts. Is the maze not possible? Easily fixed.

Finally, you can ink your maze by tracing your lines with a fine point marker or pen. Be careful not to close up any doorways!

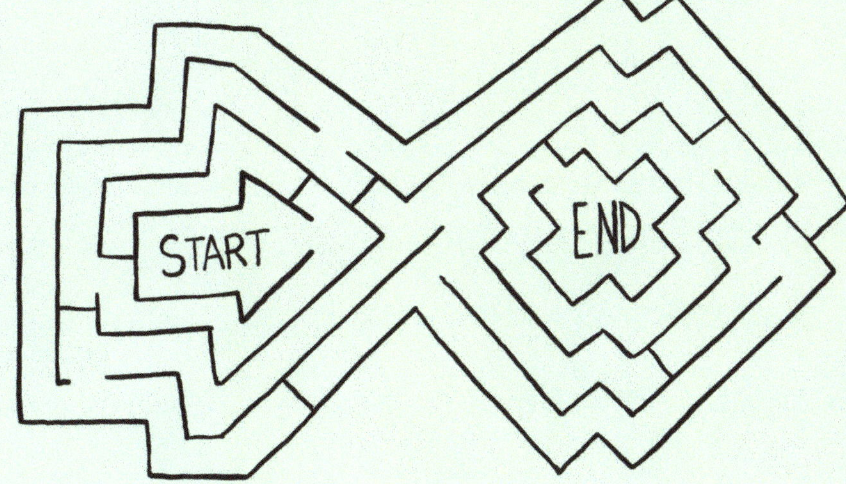


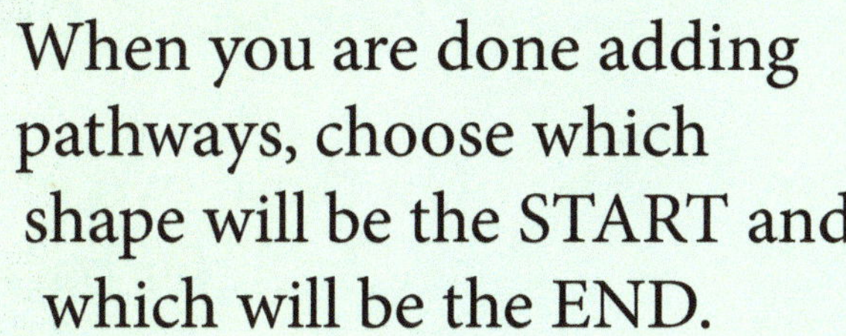
THE Seltzer METHOD

# Make your own mazes using two shapes

On these two pages, make a maze using two shapes as seeds. Refer back to the previous pages if you get stuck. Choose any two simple shapes, such as a circle, a star, a square, a heart, and so on.



**Making Mazes** LESSONS, CHALLENGES, & WORKBOOK

# One complex shape as a seed

This maze has one seed that looks like four. Treat it like you would treat a single shape.

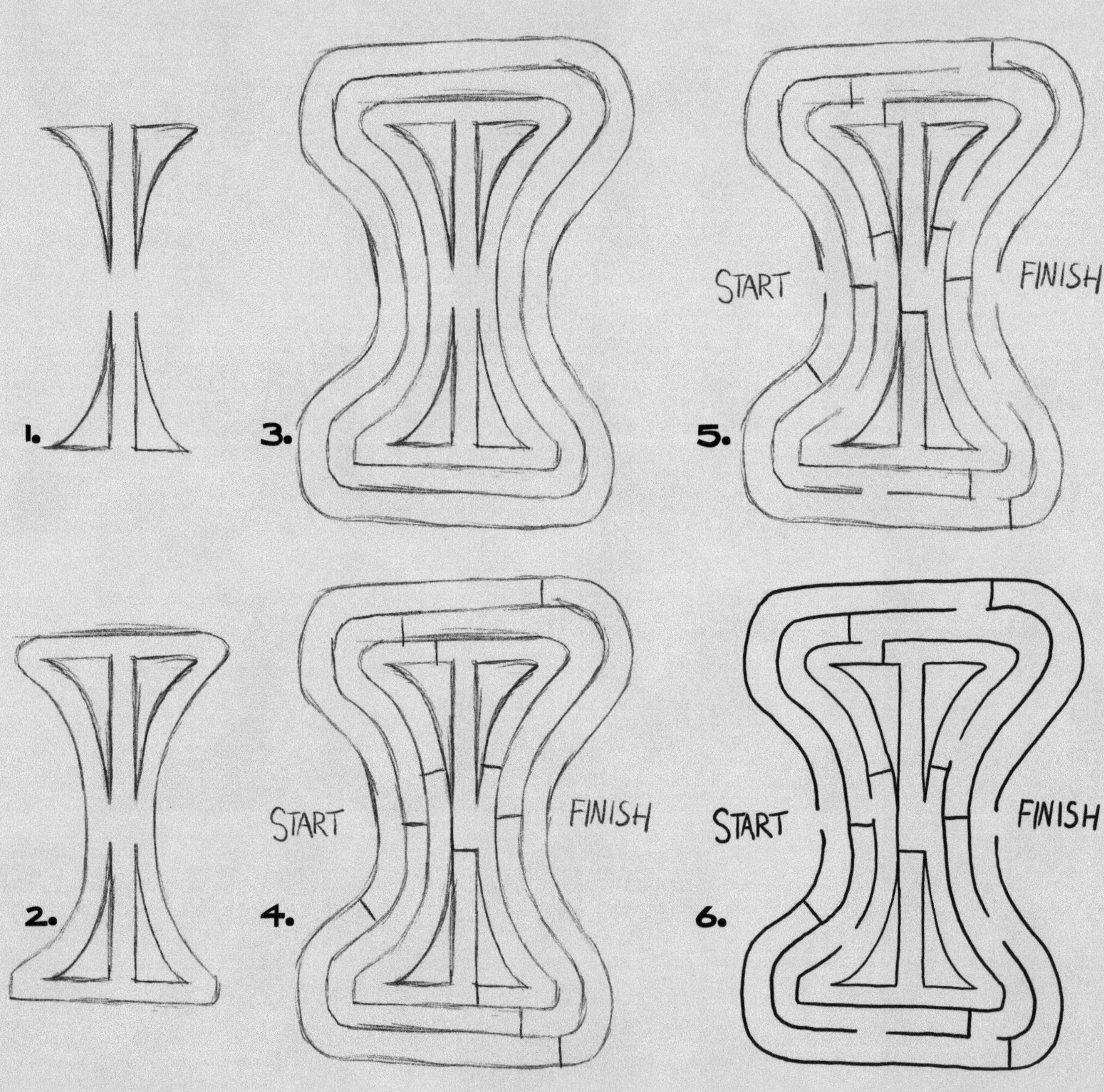



 **Making Mazes** LESSONS, CHALLENGES, & WORKBOOK

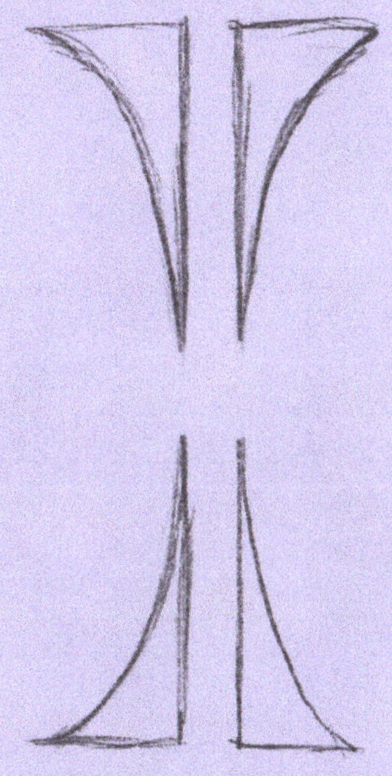

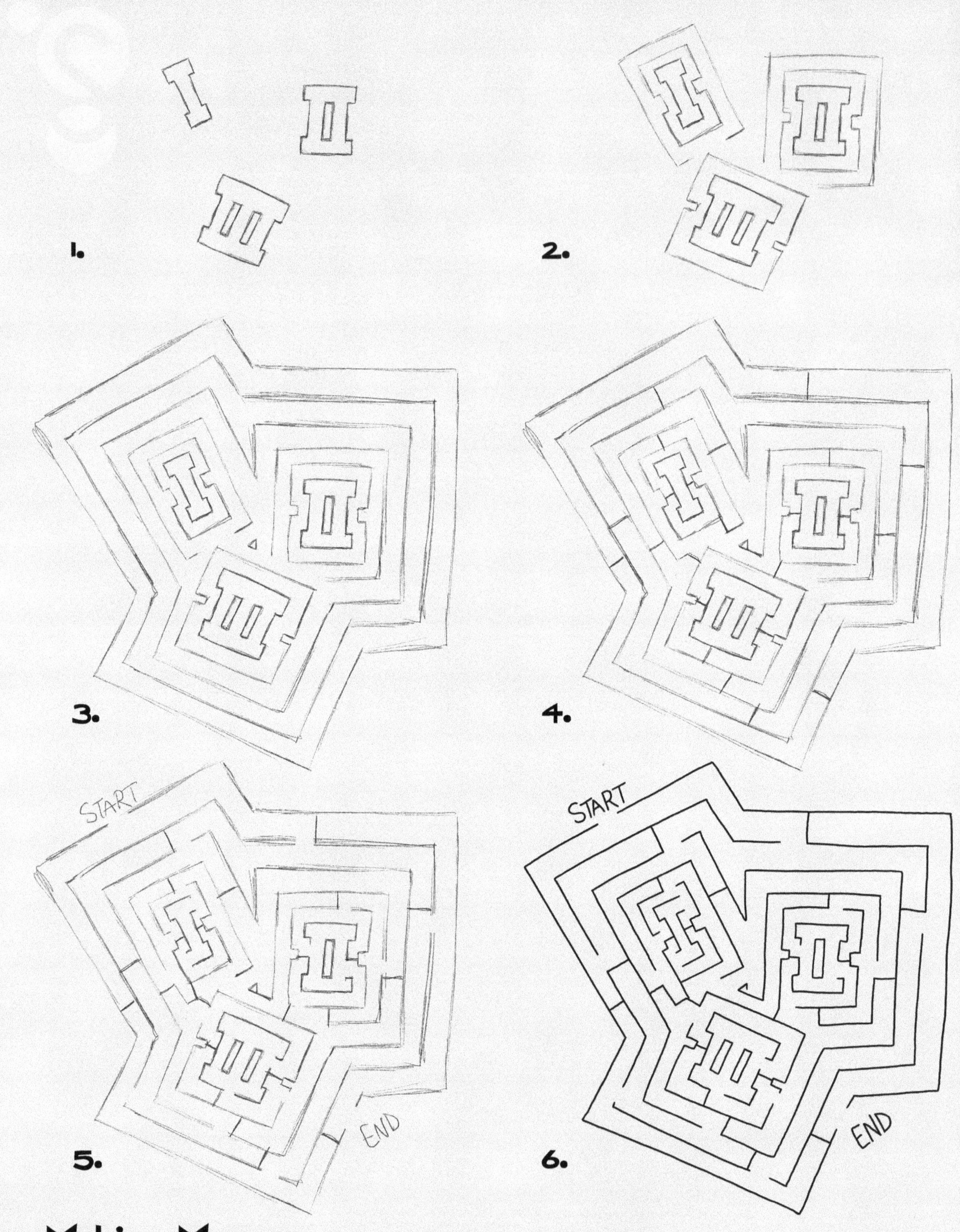


**1.**

**2.**

**3.**

**4.**

**5.**

**6.**



# Making Mazes LESSONS, CHALLENGES, & WORKBOOK

# Three Seeds

Now try making a maze using these three seed shapes.
Your maze doesn't need to look like the example.

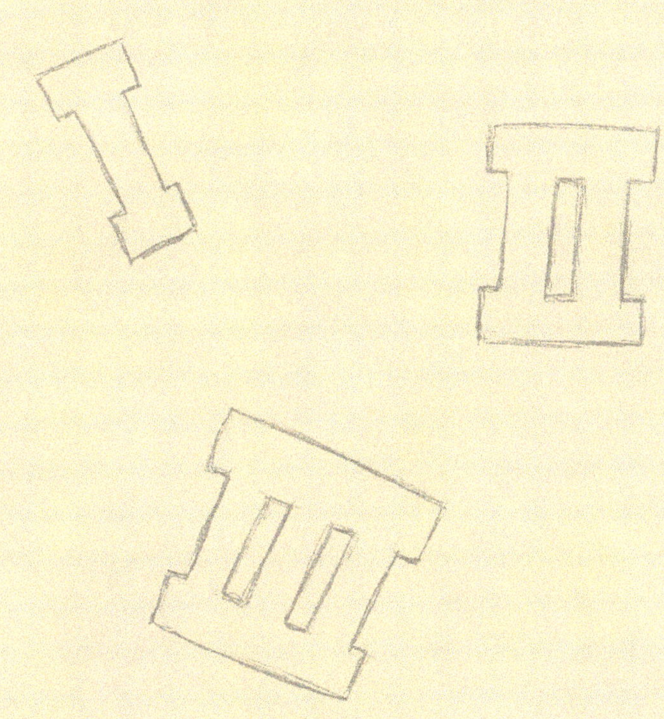

# WORD

WORD

WORD



**Making Mazes** LESSONS, CHALLENGES, & WORKBOOK

# Using words to make mazes

Letters are simple shapes. Just like other shapes, they can be used as the seeds of a maze. In the example to the left, the letters are make up of a single line. The pathways are built around them. Try writing your initials below using the same kind of letters and make a maze from them.

WORD

WORD

WORD



**Making Mazes** LESSONS, CHALLENGES, & WORKBOOK

# Using words to make mazes... continued.

These letters are more complicated than the ones on the
previous page. The letters are outlined and the thickness
of the letters are the same size as the pathways. In fact, the
letters can be broken into and used as part of the maze.
Can you make letters like this? Try it out below.

# Three shape maze

These three toadstools, and their winged visitor, make three shapes. These shapes are the seeds for your maze. Make pathways around them and allow them to grow together into one big maze.

See how Jerry finished this maze in the Challenge section on page 61.

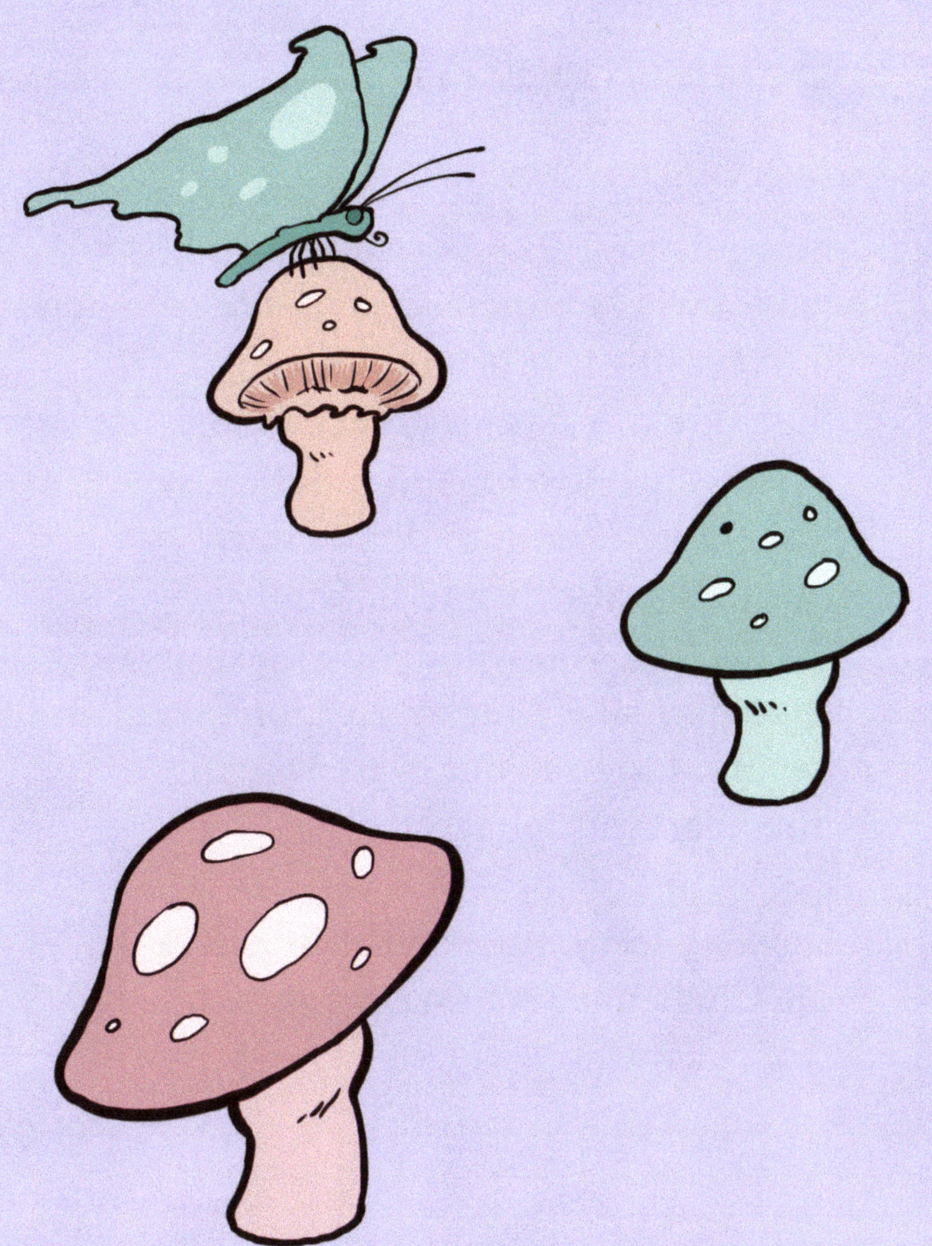

## Seven shapes!?!?

What happens when you have even more shapes? In this example you have a whole bunch of shapes to build your maze around. Some of them are too close together to put a pathway between and others have just enough room to divide into two paths. Slowly and patiently decide how you will divide up the space to make your maze. Don't be afraid to use your eraser if your lines start misbehaving.

See how Jerry finished this maze in the Challenge section on page 63.

 **Making Mazes** LESSONS, CHALLENGES, & WORKBOOK

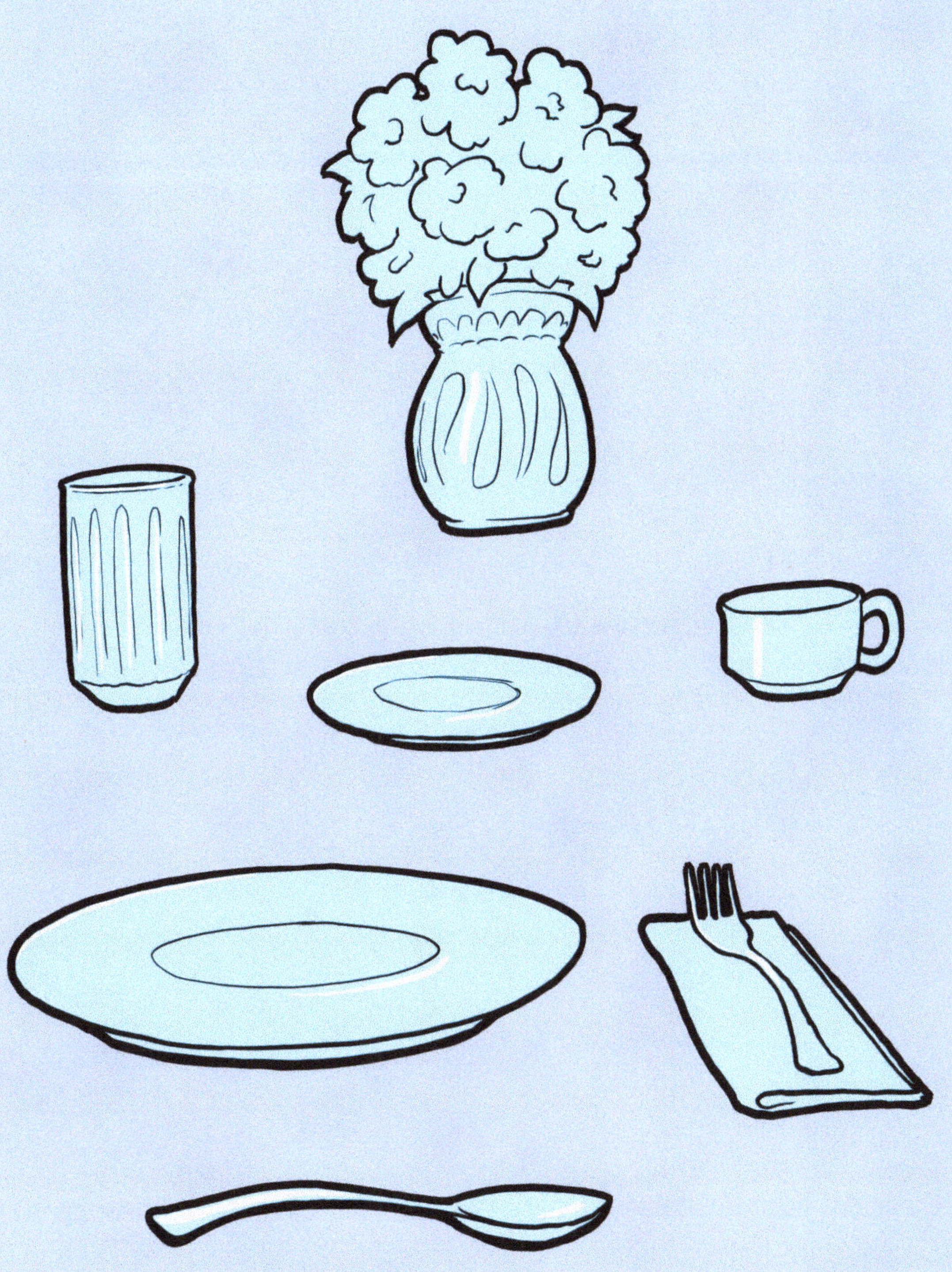

# Making a happy home

There are five shapes in this maze to get you started. Can you draw pathways around them all and bring them together? Where will your start and end be?

Keep your pathways around one centimeter wide. That is about how wide your pencil is.

See how Jerry finished this maze in the Challenge section on page 65.

 **Making Mazes** LESSONS, CHALLENGES, & WORKBOOK

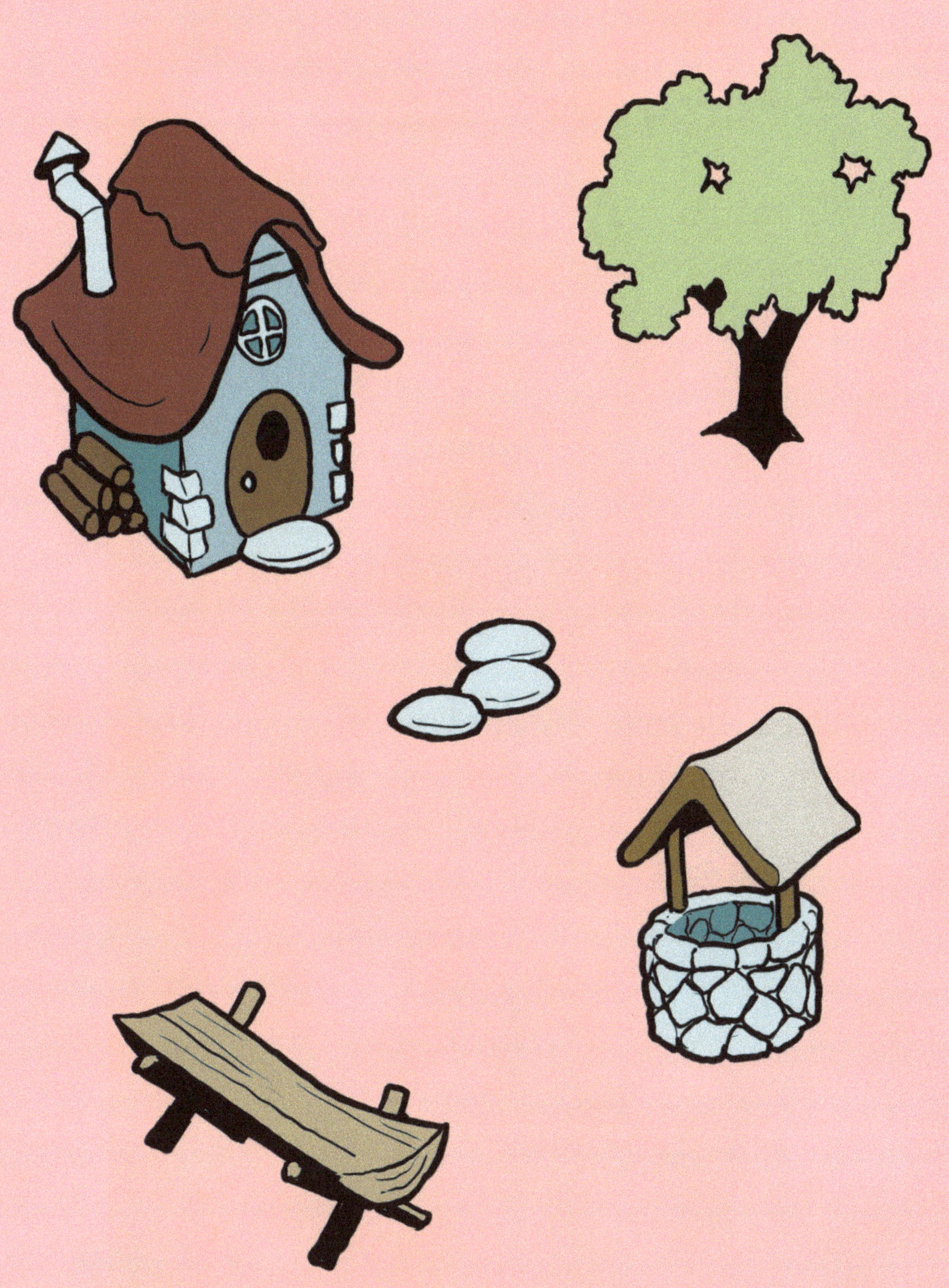

## Swampy swirls

In this maze, you begin with four shapes. Not only that, but there are also ripples in the water that are making other lines. Can you work all of those things into your maze? Take your time. If you rush, you might make a messy maze. Slow down and do the best job that you can.

See how Jerry finished this maze in the Challenge section on page 67.

 **Making Mazes** LESSONS, CHALLENGES, & WORKBOOK

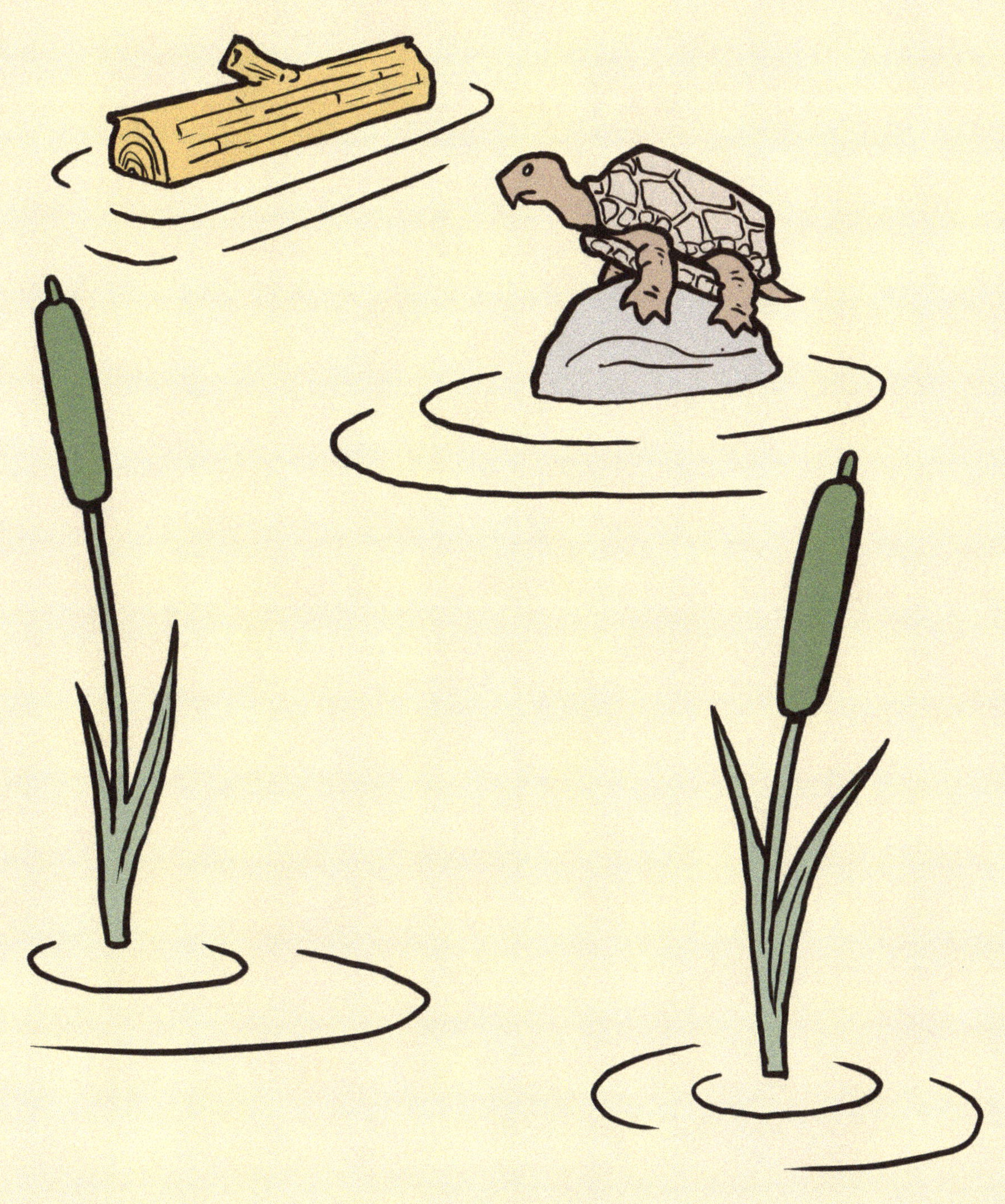

THE Seltzer METHOD  27

# Comfy quilty cozy maze

In this maze, you will need to work inside of a shape instead of outside. Be careful not to let your pathways get too narrow. Take your time and be patient. Remember to test your pencil-drawn maze before you start inking it.

See how Jerry finished this maze in the Challenge section on page 69.

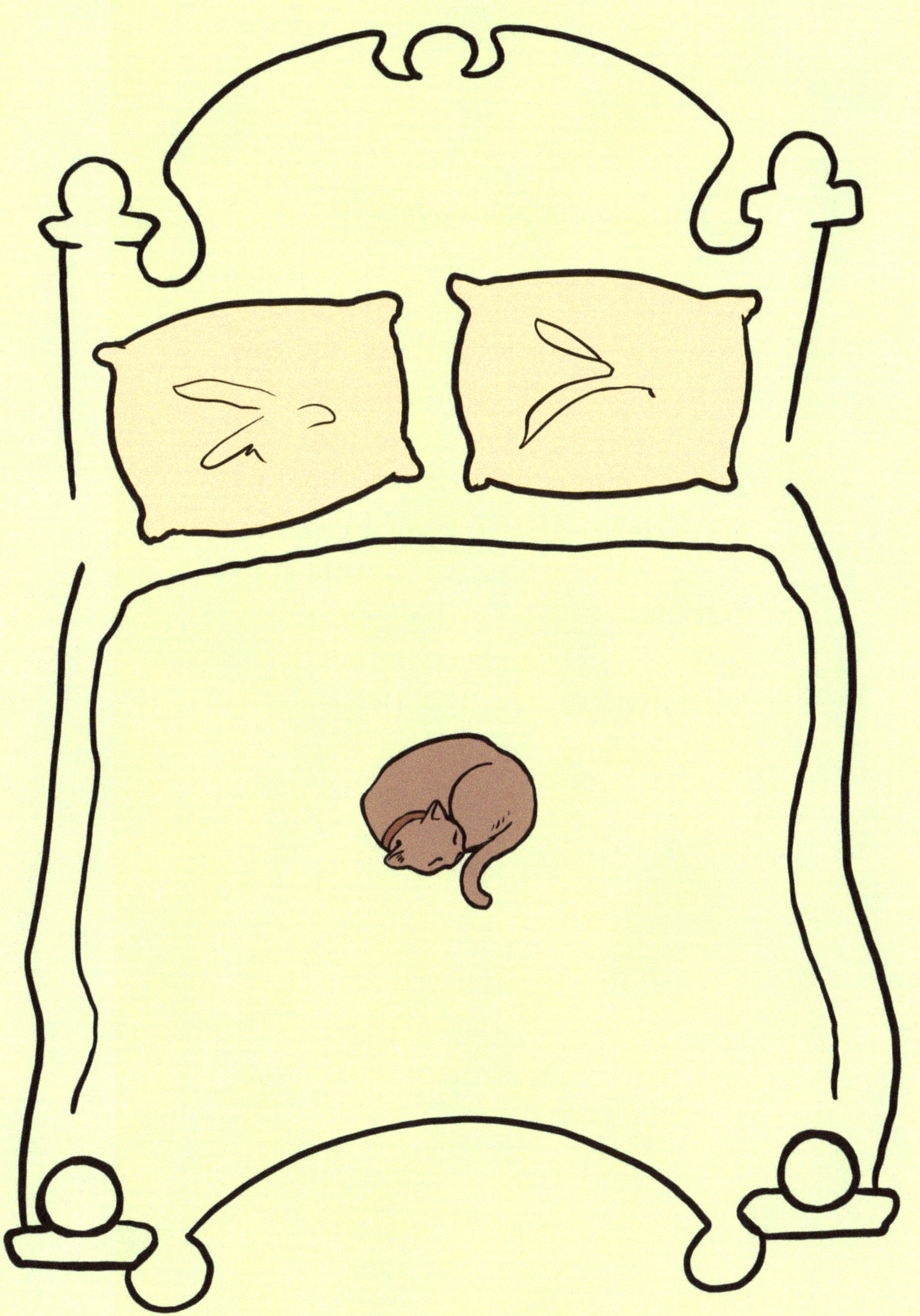

THE Seltzer METHOD 29

# The lab experiment

Scientists have learned a lot about how brains work by observing rats in mazes. If you build the rest of this maze, how fast do you think your parent or sibling could get to the cheese? Maybe you can make copies of your maze and time your "rats" to see who is the fastest.

See how Jerry finished this maze in the Challenge section on page 71.

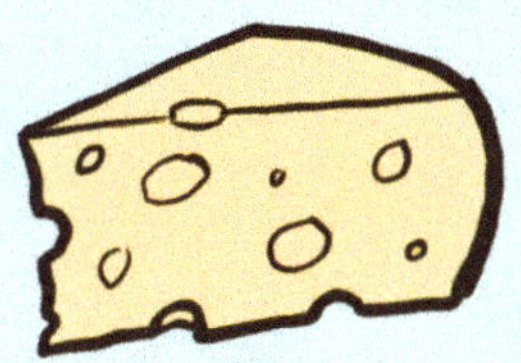

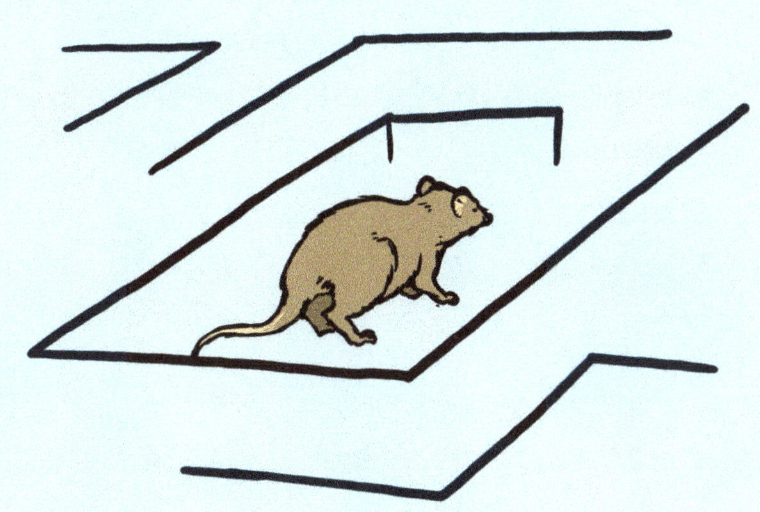

# Three Keys To Exit

The seeds to this maze are keys. Before anyone can exit the maze, they must first find each of the three keys. Don't make it too easy for them!

What other items could a person collect as they are completing a maze? They might grab the ingredients of a meal or the parts of an invention or the letters to their name. What other ideas can you come up with?

See how Jerry finished this maze in the Challenge section on page 73.

 **Making Mazes** LESSONS, CHALLENGES, & WORKBOOK

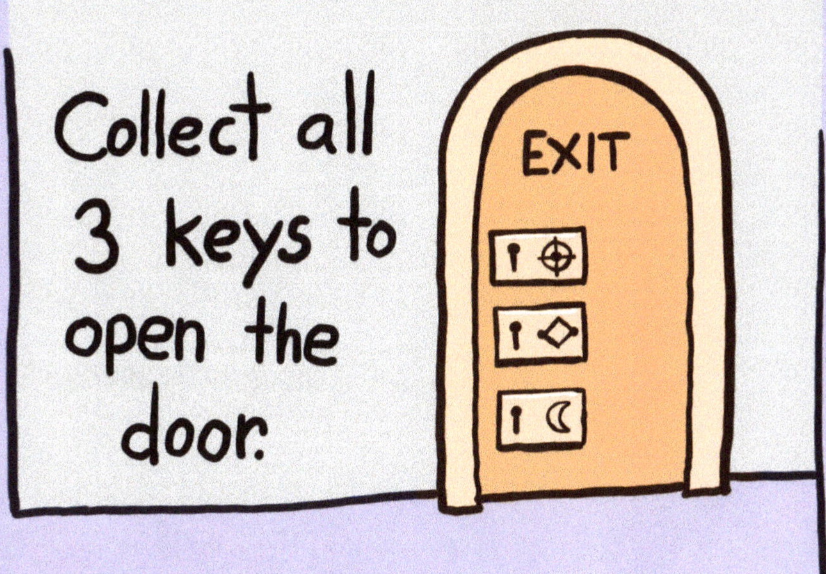

Collect all
3 keys to
open the
door.
EXIT


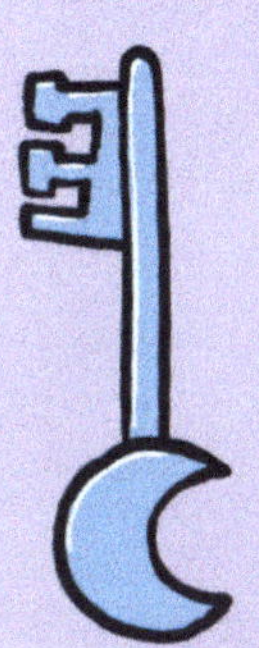

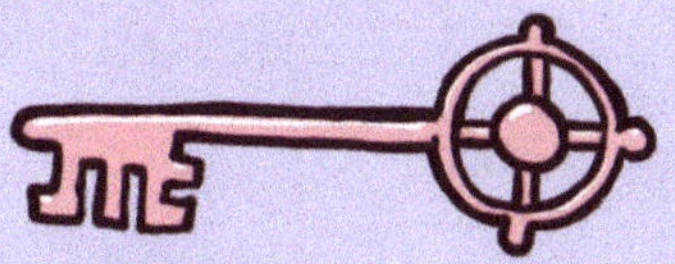

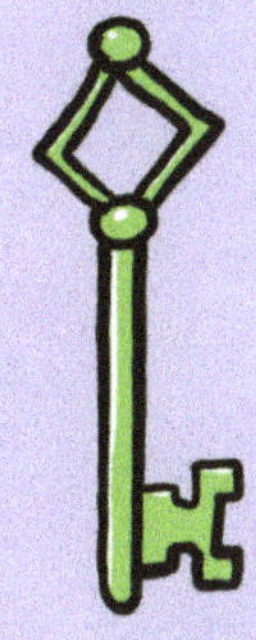


THE Seltzer METHOD

## The Pirate Puzzle

Waves make a certain kind of line
in the water. For this maze, you
have been given a few wave lines
to get you started. Can you make a
tricky maze while keeping the seas
calm? Or are the pirates on the ship
going to get seasick?

See how Jerry finished this maze in
the Challenge section on page 75.

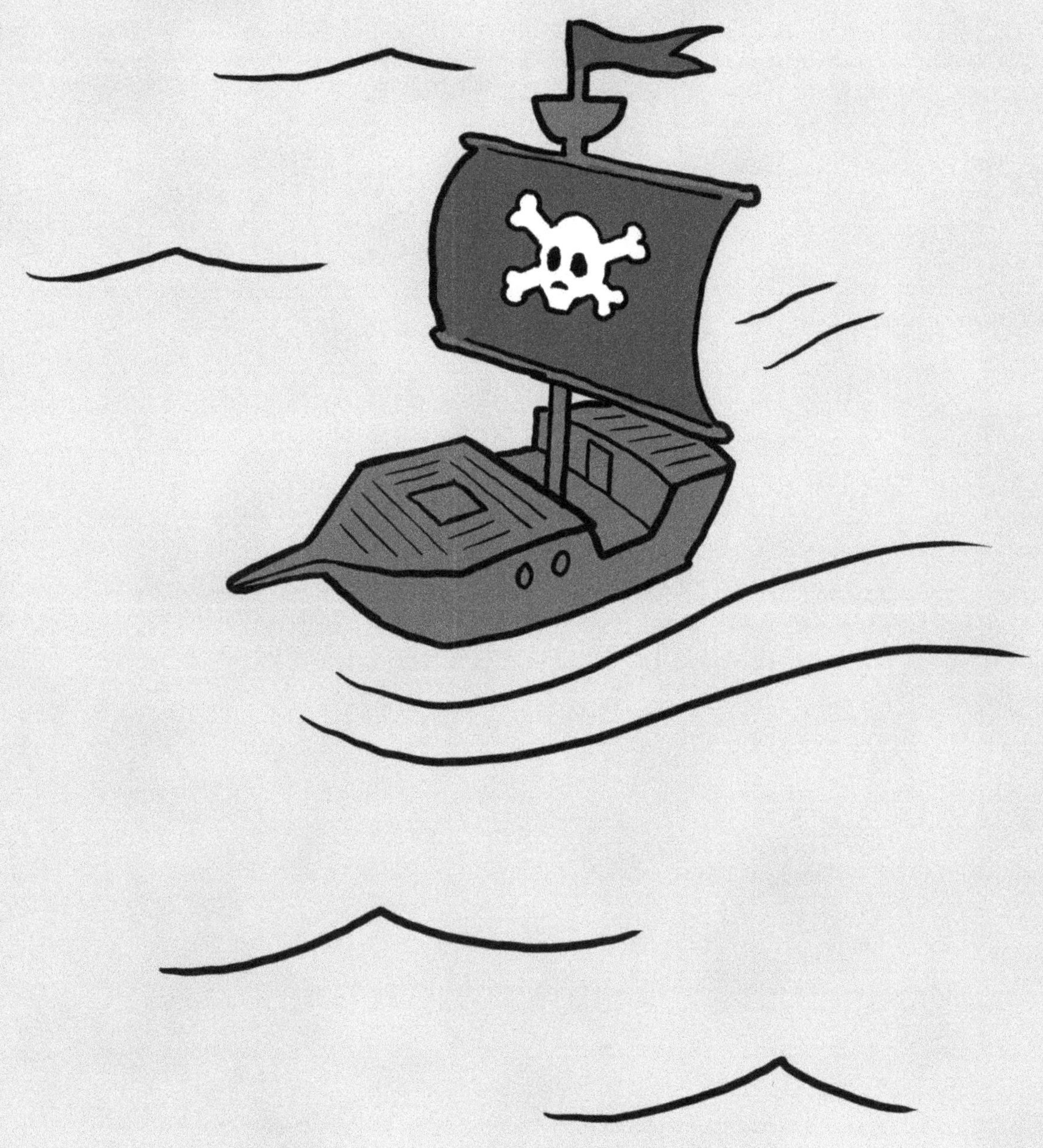

THE Seltzer METHOD 35

# An amazing bouquet

These flowers are blooming into an interesting pattern. Can you build upon the seed provided to finish this maze? What other flower shapes can you add? Perhaps a bee needs to navigate through the maze, pollinating the flowers as she goes?

See how Jerry finished this maze in the Challenge section on page 77.

 **Making Mazes** LESSONS, CHALLENGES, & WORKBOOK

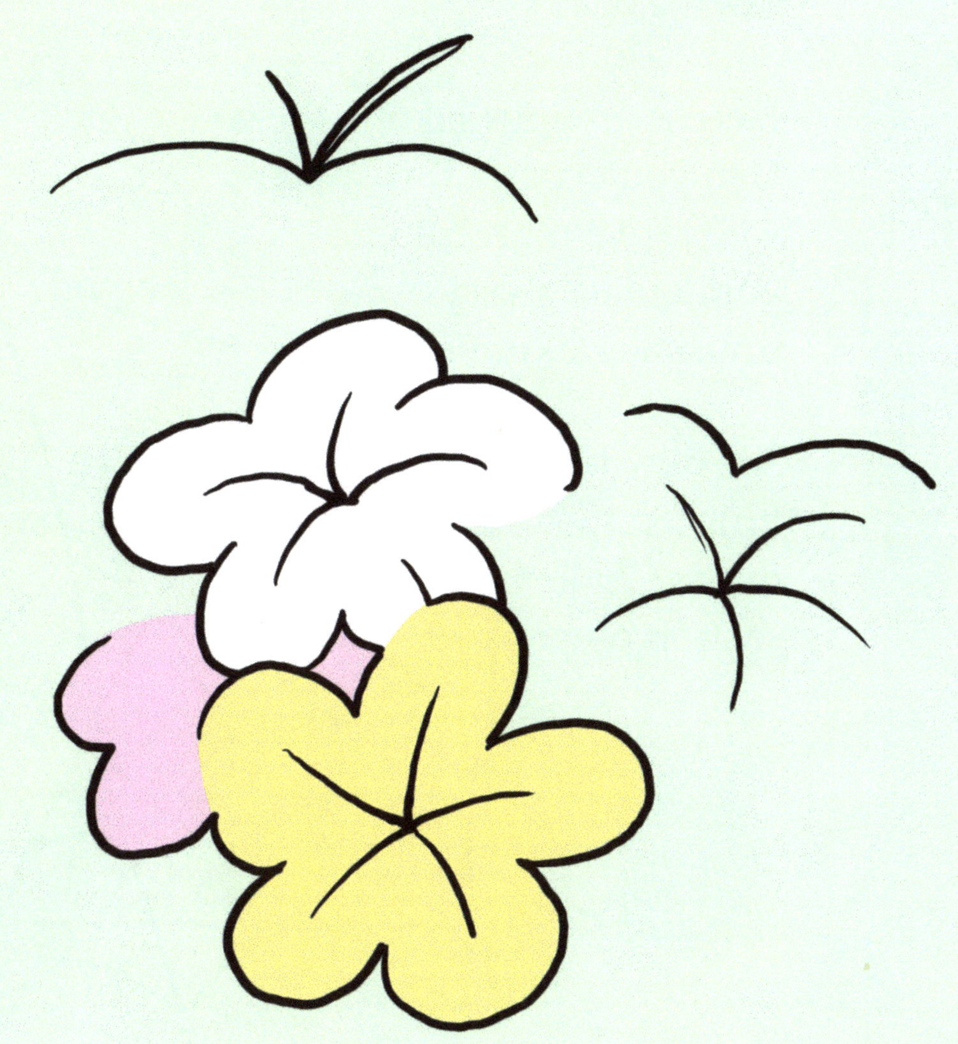

## Caught up in a web of confusion

Here is an unusual one for you. Can you expand this spider's web into a maze? It is going to be a very unusual looking web.

See how Jerry finished this maze in the Challenge section on page 79.

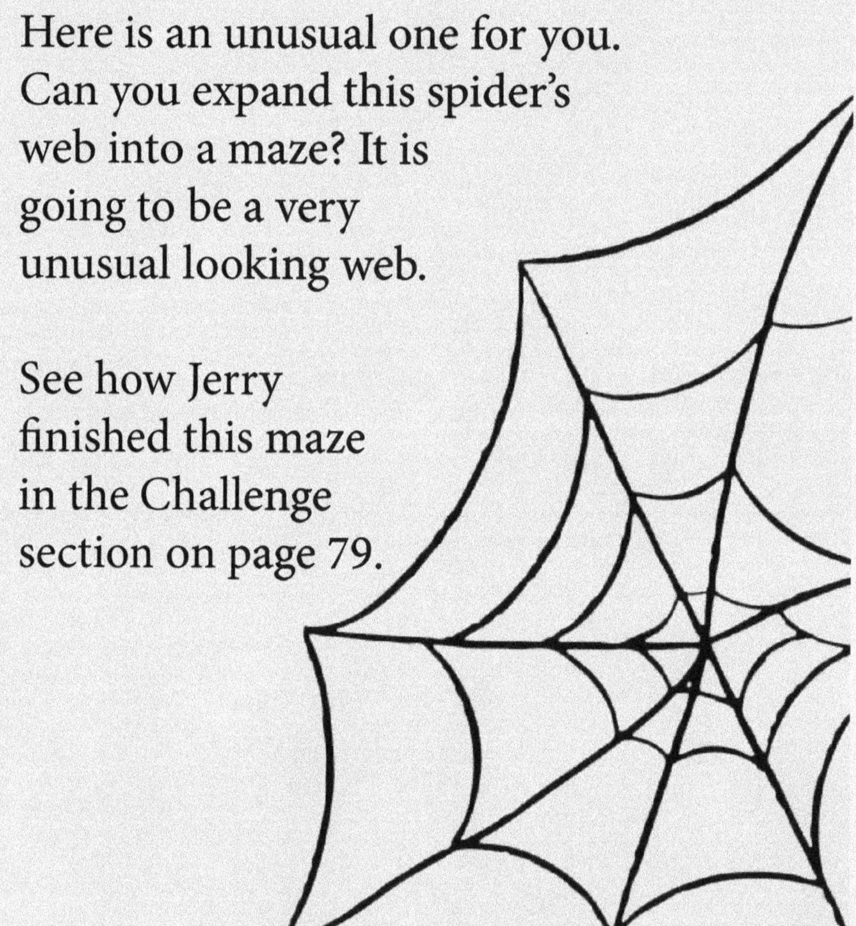

 **Making Mazes**  LESSONS, CHALLENGES, & WORKBOOK

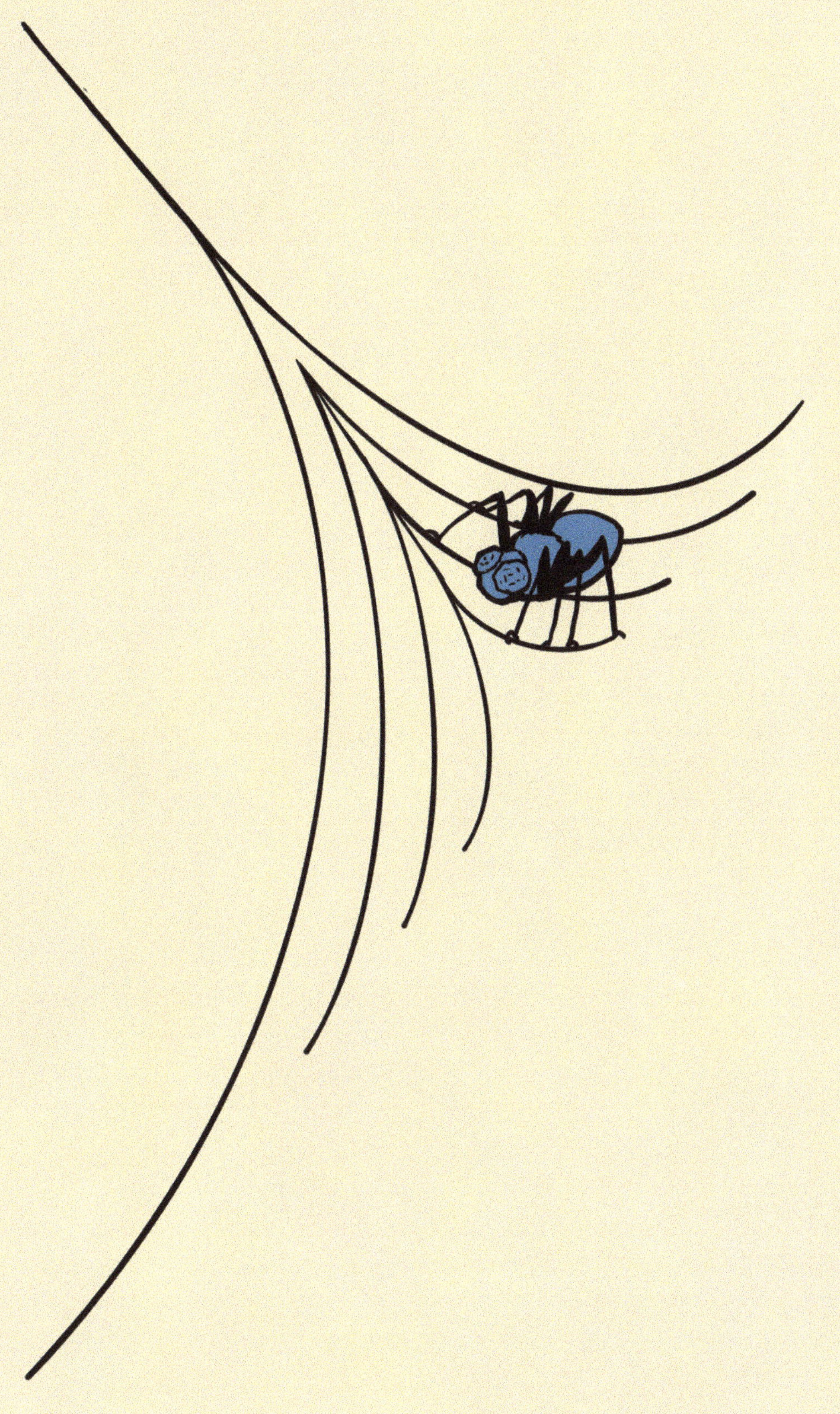

THE Seltzer METHOD 39

# A Maze of Branches

If you were a squirrel, you might see a tree like a maze. There are branches twisting and turning, some that reach to the next tree, and some that are dead ends. To complete the tree maze shown here, use branches and leaves to make challenging  path to the ground. Don't let your branches get too thin. In the trunk area, use lines in the bark as the walls of your maze.

See how Jerry finished this maze in the Challenge section on page 81.

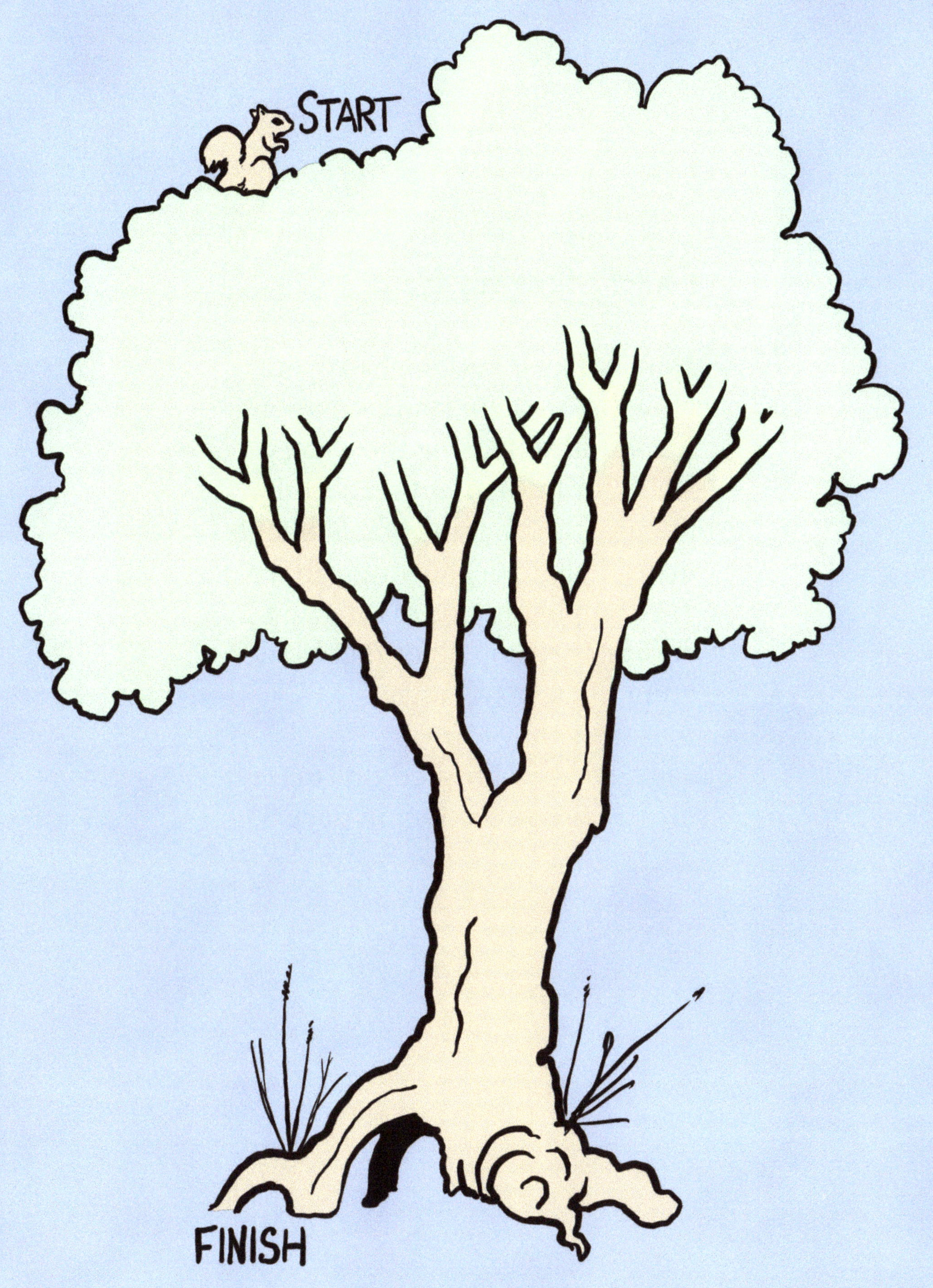


THE Seltzer METHOD 41

# Fluidly flowing fences

Here is a new challenge for you. How can we depict an undersea scene without losing the watery feel? Our lines might section the picture into uncomfortable bubbles instead of gentle, flowing, currents. Try completing this maze using curling, swirling, lines that branch off in unexpected ways.

See how Jerry finished this maze in the Challenge section on page 83.

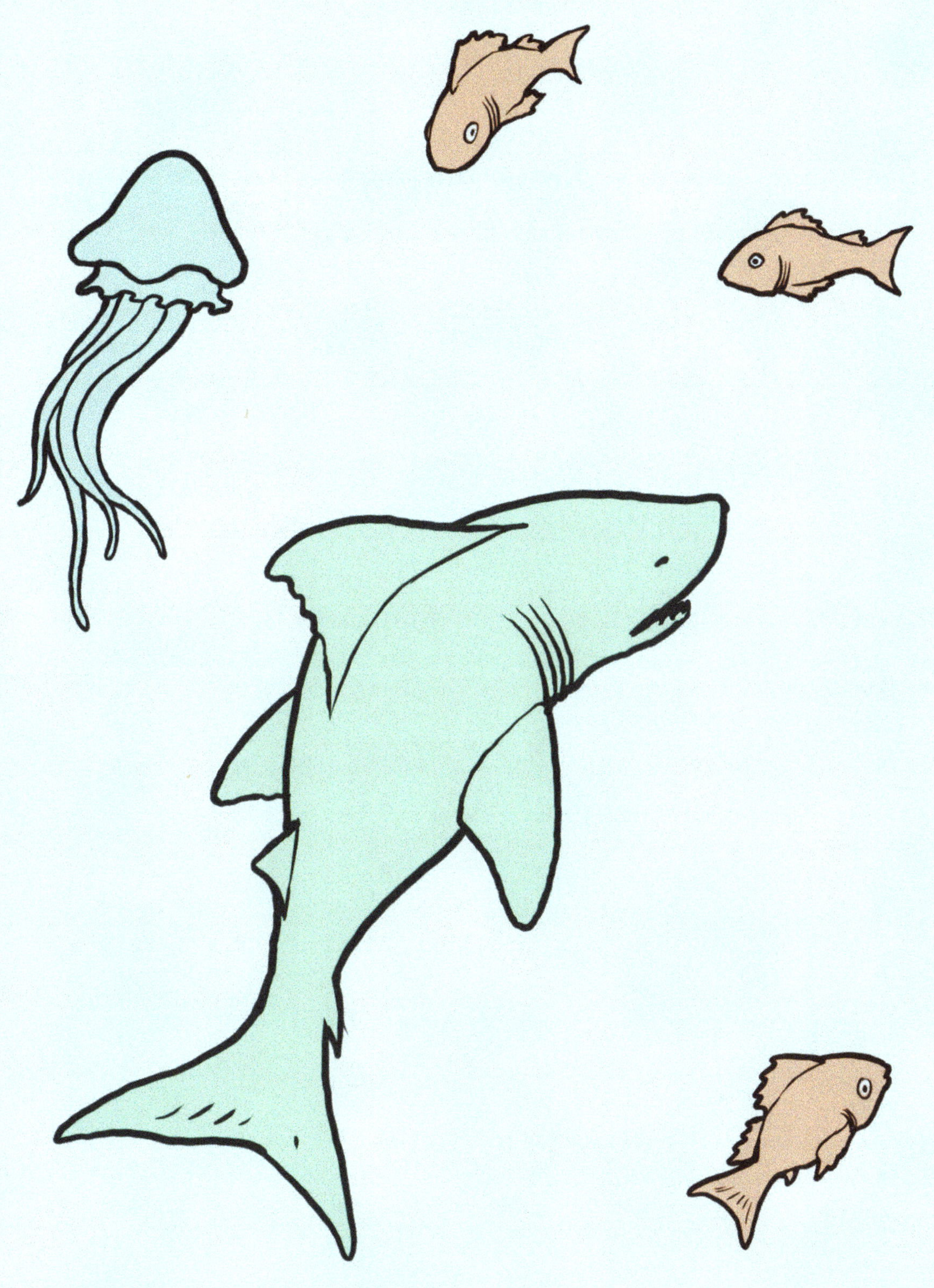

## With a little imagination, a maze can be an adventure!

The hero is coming to slay the dragon, who is asleep in its lair. The hero will need to find the magic sword and the magic shield before facing the dragon. Use the dragon, the sword, and the shield just as you would use any three shapes to begin a maze.

See how Jerry finished this maze in the Challenge section on page 85.

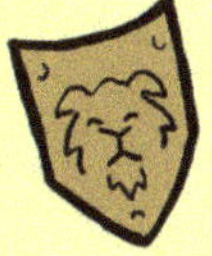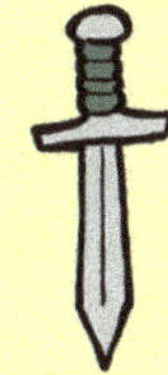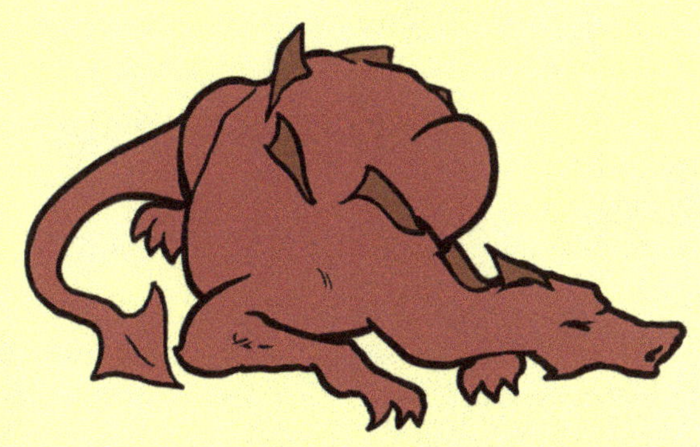

## Can you make a maze based on a video game?

Here is the seed of maze based on the Pac Man video game. The goal is to gather all the white dots without running into the ghosts. Once you have all the dots, you can exit. The ghosts don't chase after you like they do in the game so for our purposes, they are really just walls. Can you finish this maze? Is there another video game you could use as the theme for a maze?

See how Jerry finished this maze in the Challenge section on page 87.

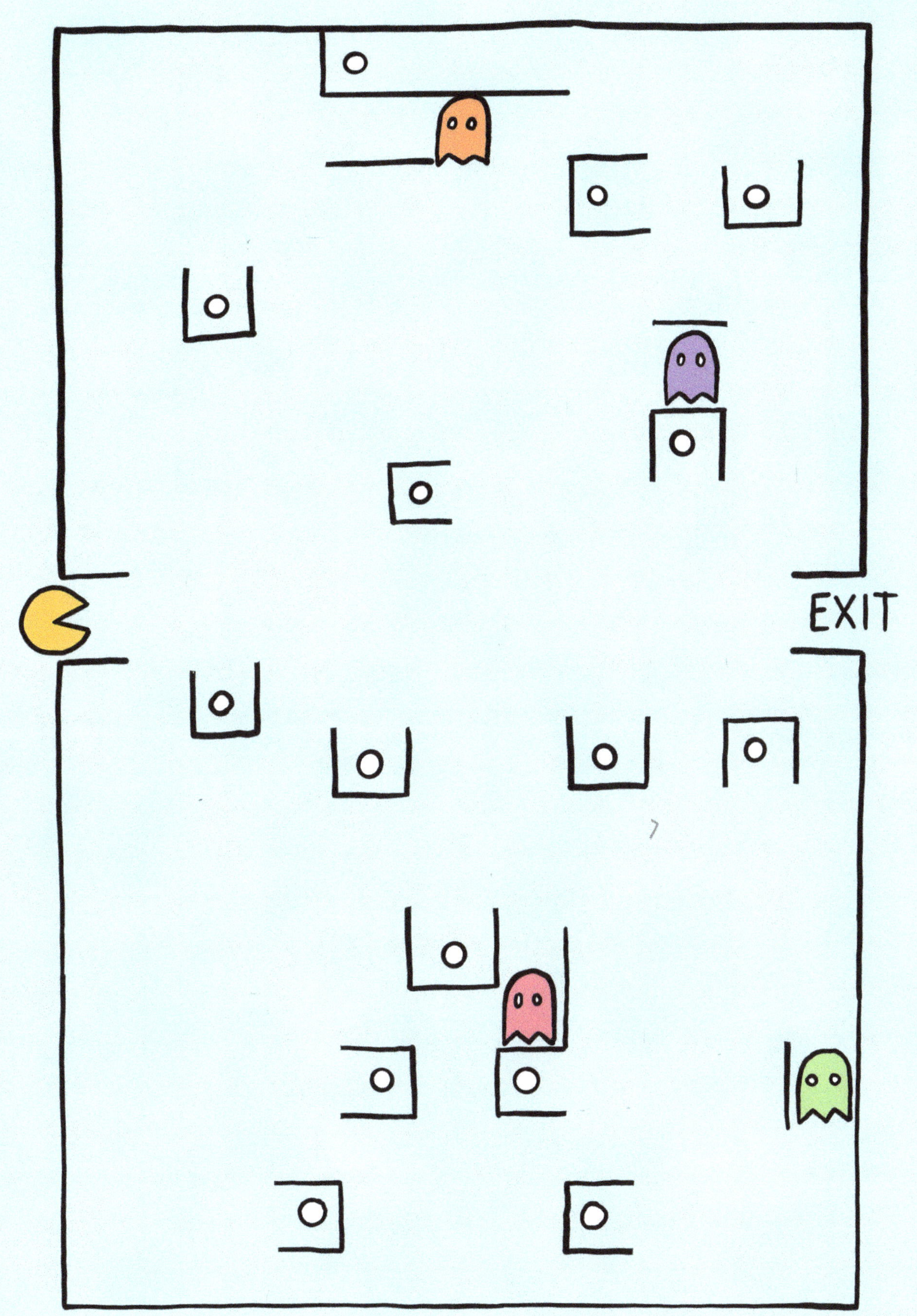

EXIT

## Lost in Suburbia

Some neighborhoods can feel like mazes. Roads, sidewalks, and fences are the lines we try to stay inside. Use the seed shapes provided to make your own neighborhood maze. What will the goal be? To get out? Or in? Or perhaps the goal is to get from your house to your friend's house. There is no wrong answer.

See how Jerry finished this maze in the Challenge section on page 89.



**Making Mazes**  LESSONS, CHALLENGES, & WORKBOOK

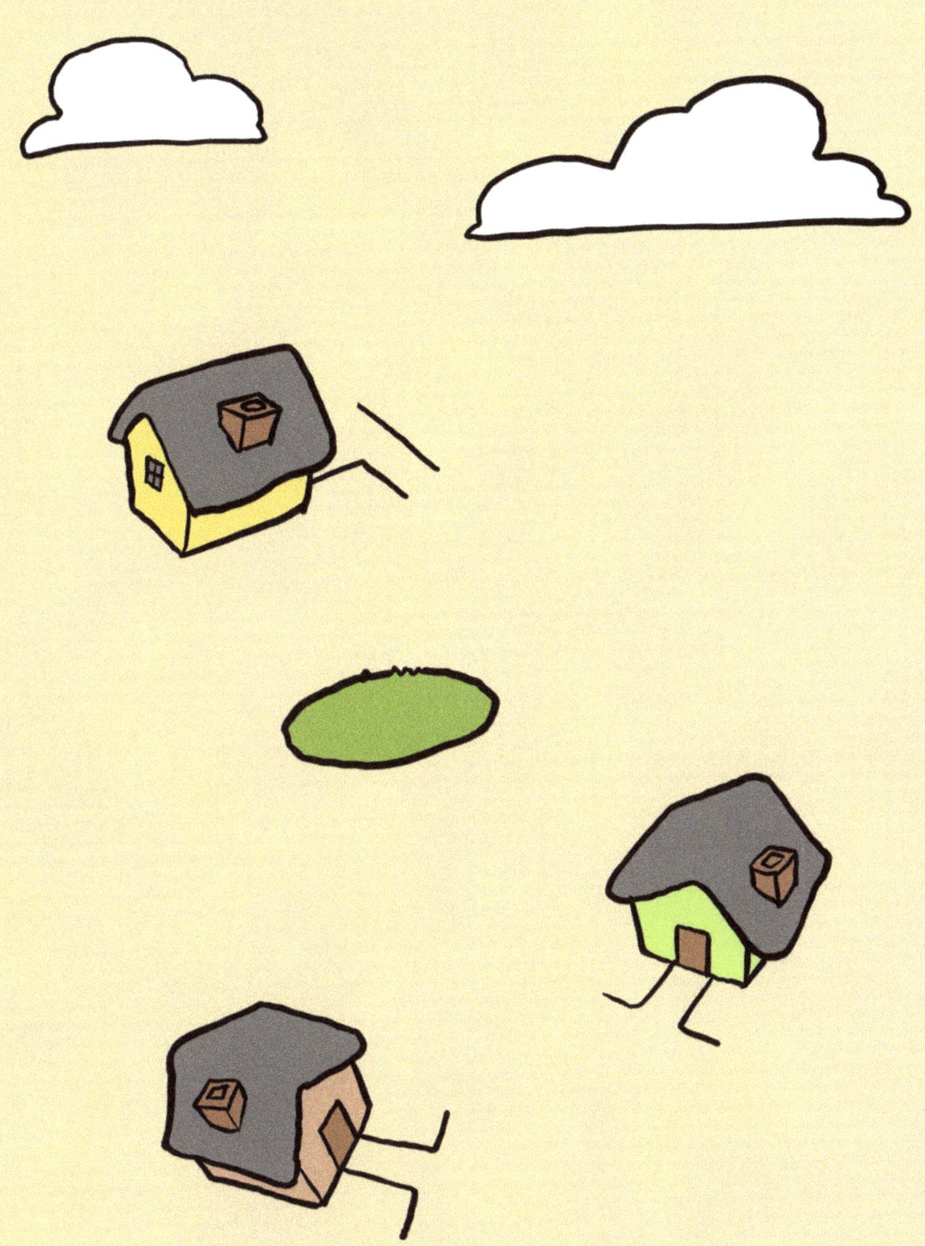

THE Seltzer METHOD

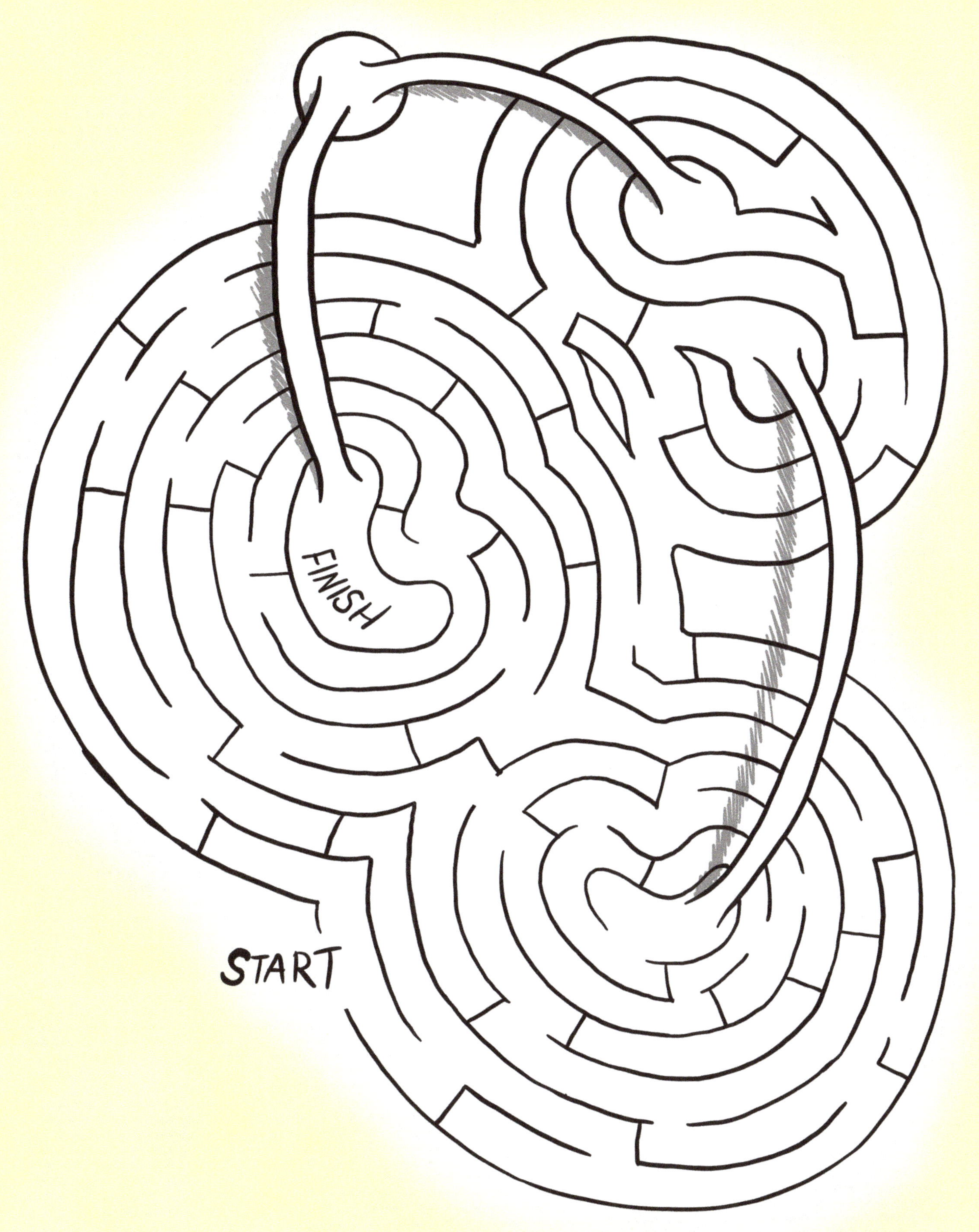

FINISH
START

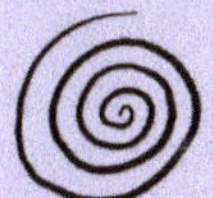 *When you reach the portal, you teleport over to the other portal.*

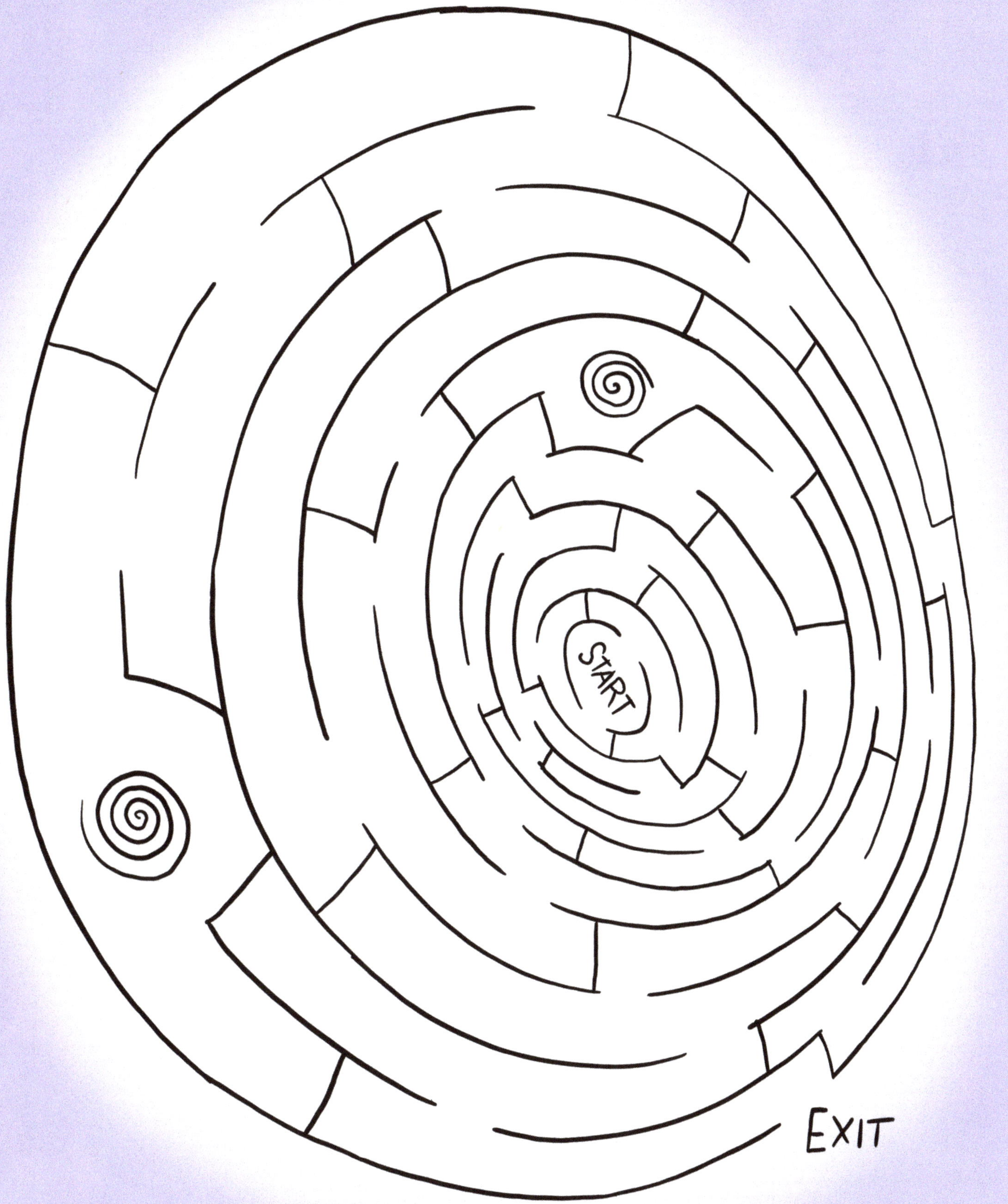

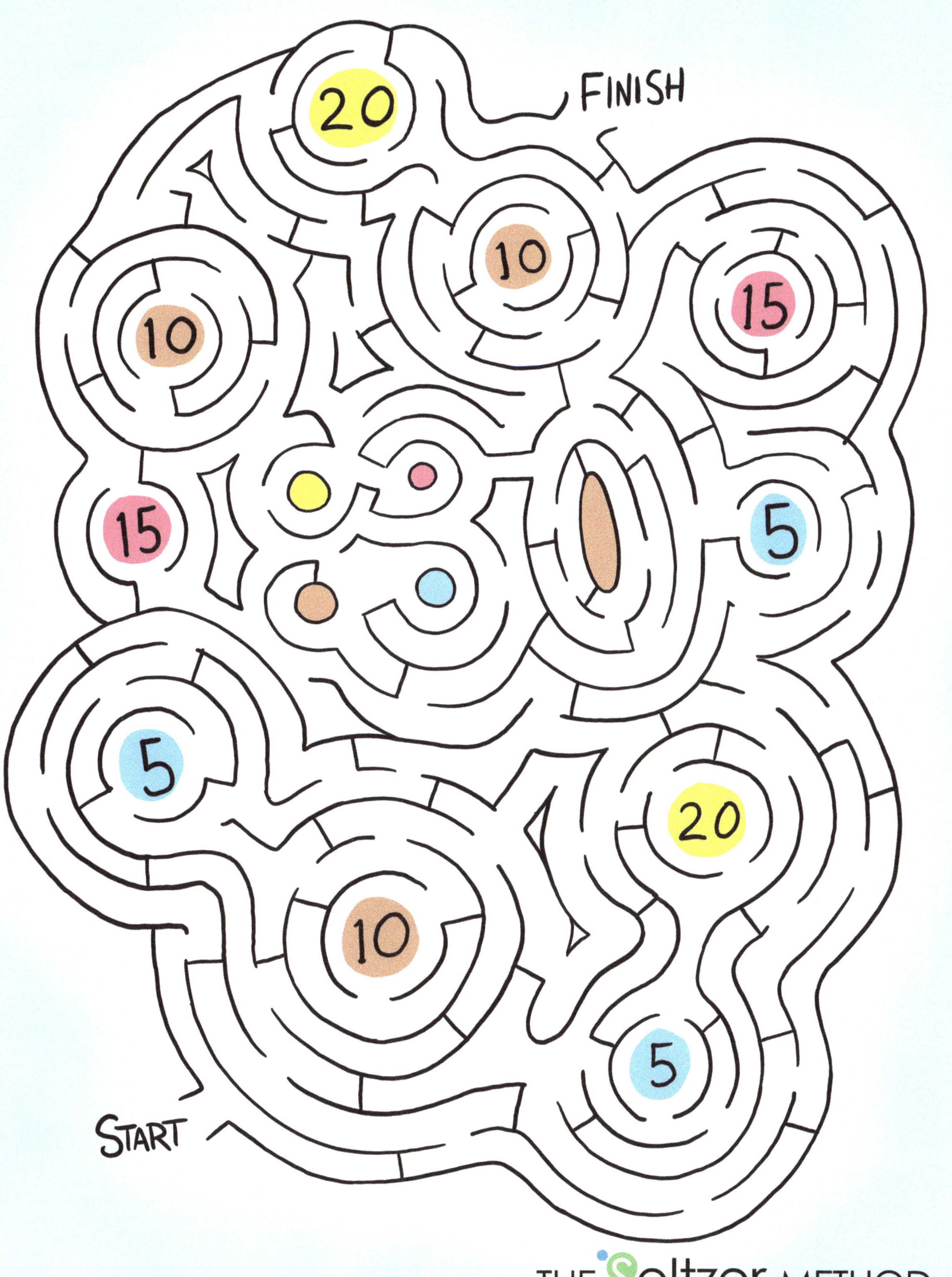

FINISH
20
10
15
10
15
5
5
20
10
5
START

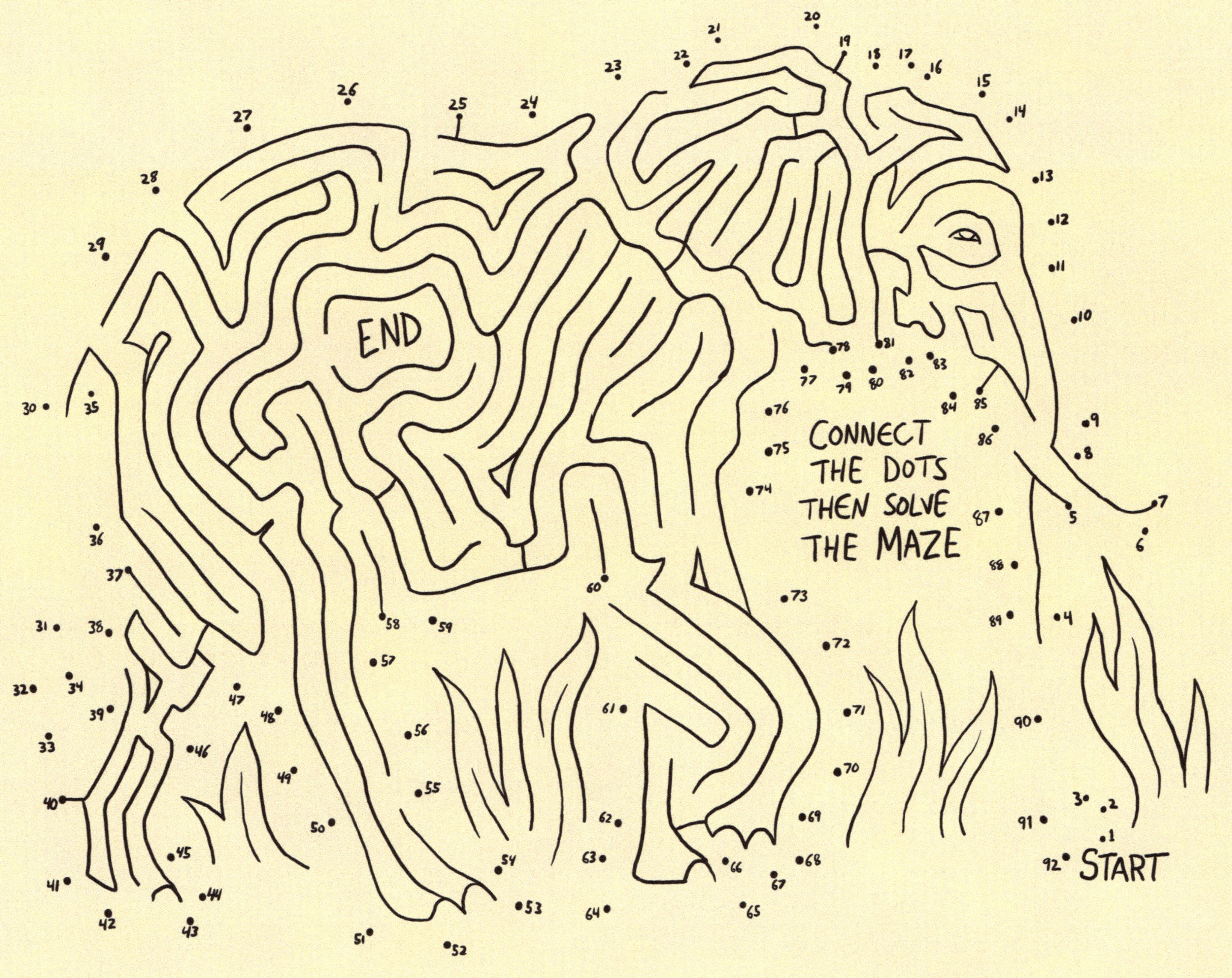

END
CONNECT THE DOTS THEN SOLVE THE MAZE
START

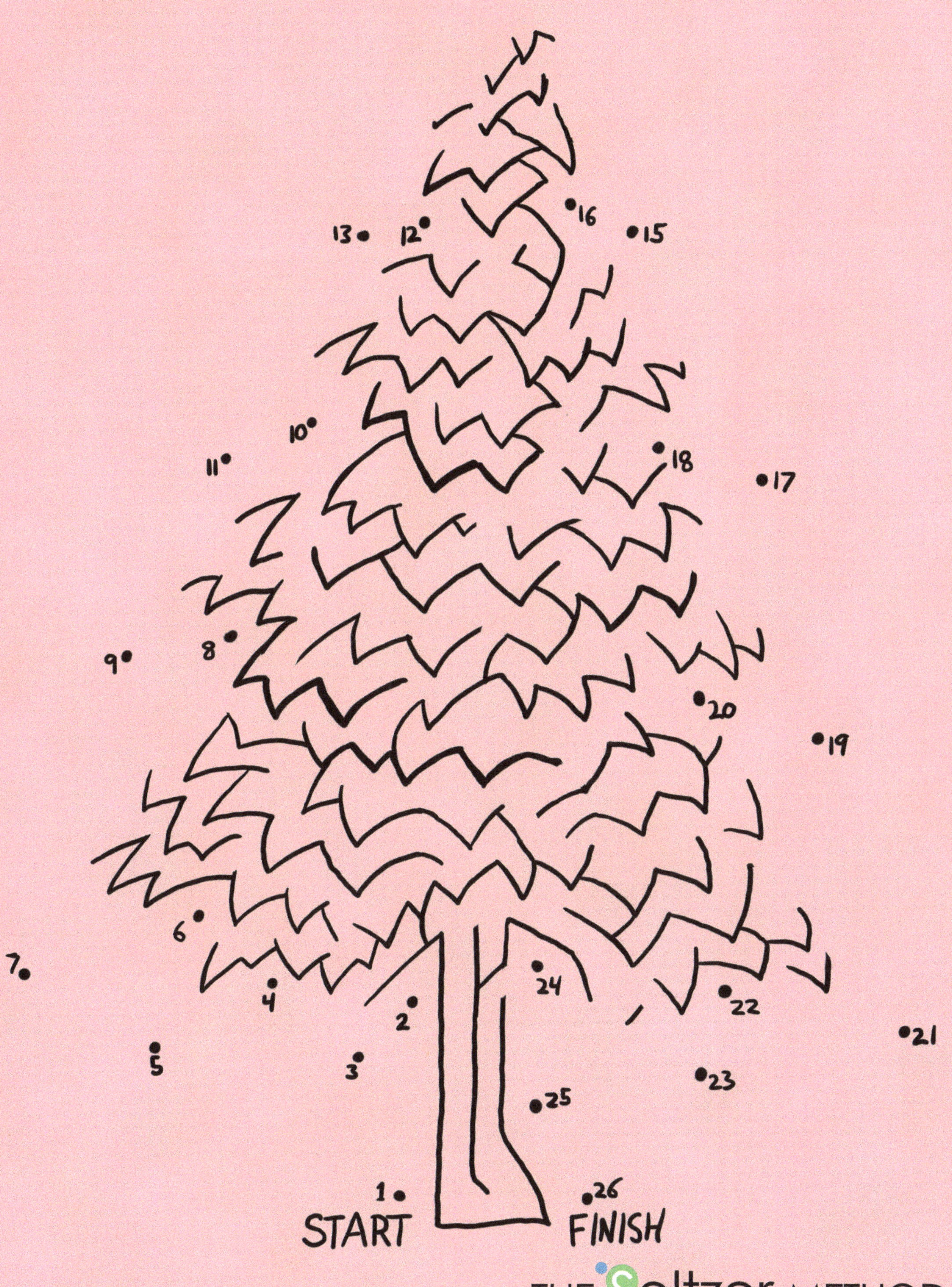

14
13  12  16  15
10
11
18
17
9  8
20
19
6
7
4
2
24
22
21
5
3
23
25
1  26
START  FINISH
THE Seltzer METHOD
59

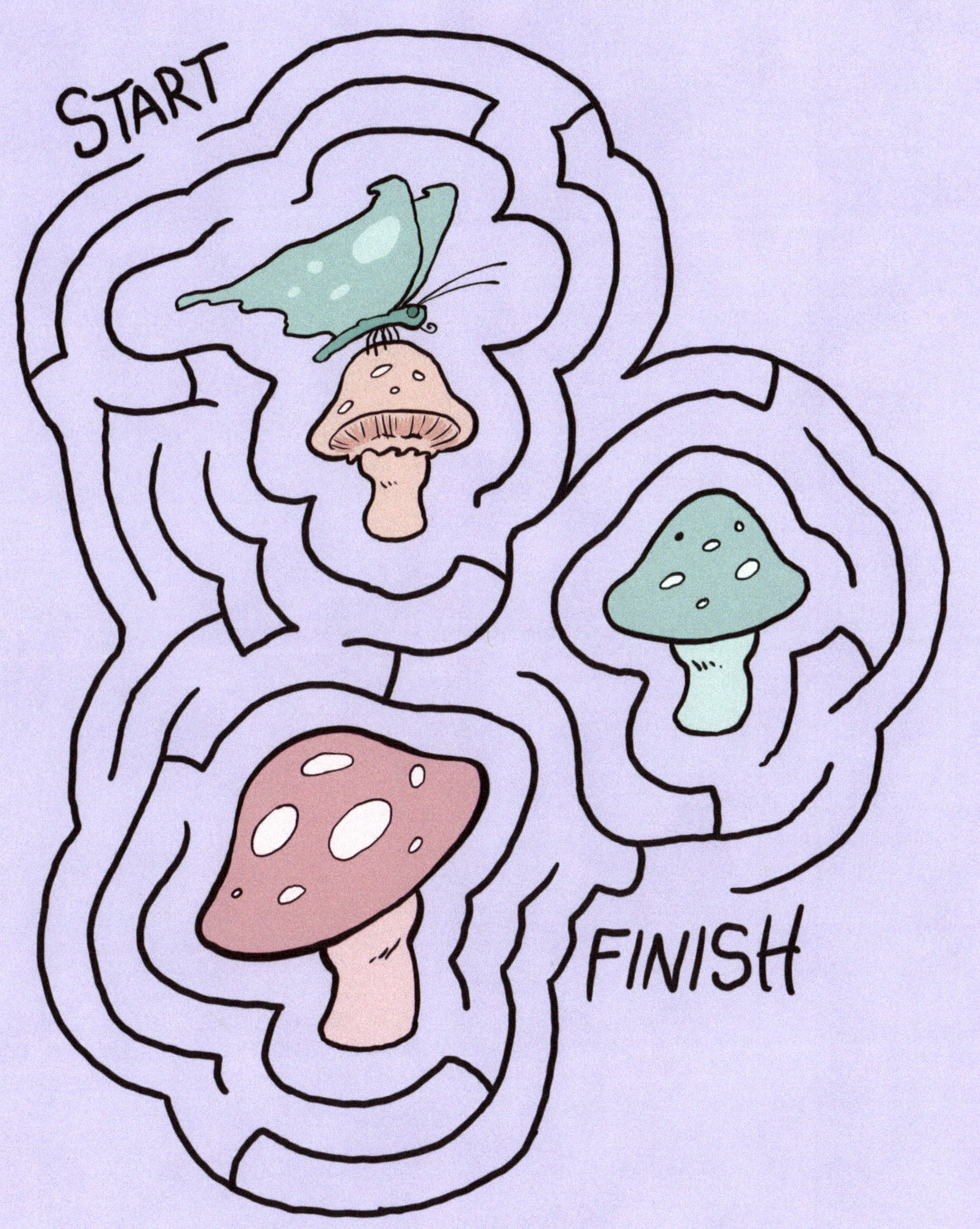

START
FINISH
THE SELTZER METHOD

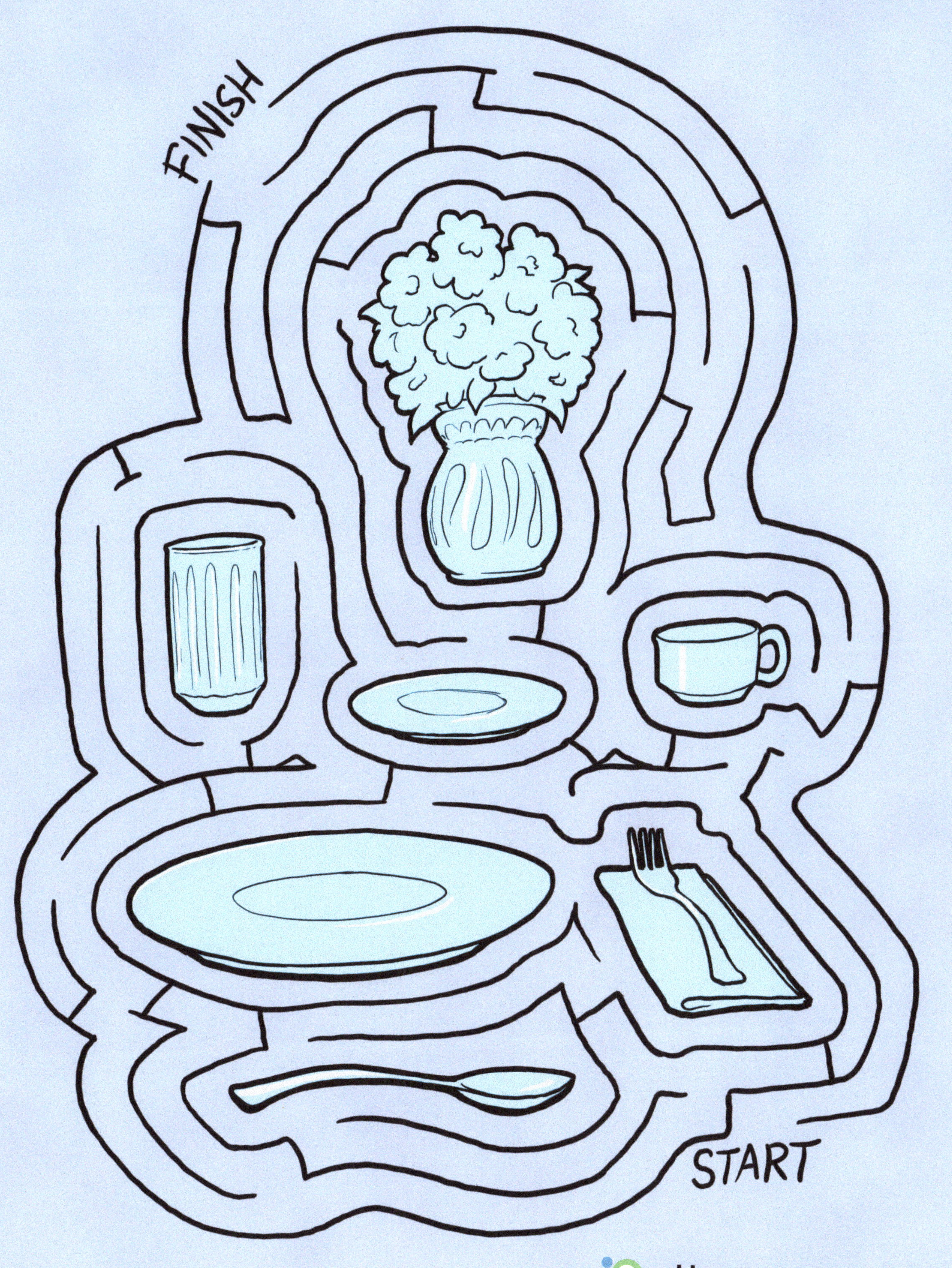

FINISH
START
THE Seltzer METHOD
63

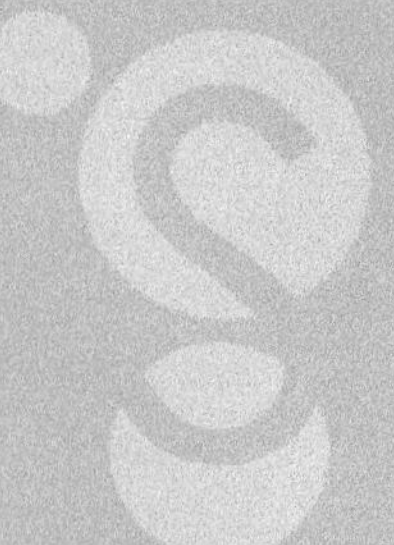

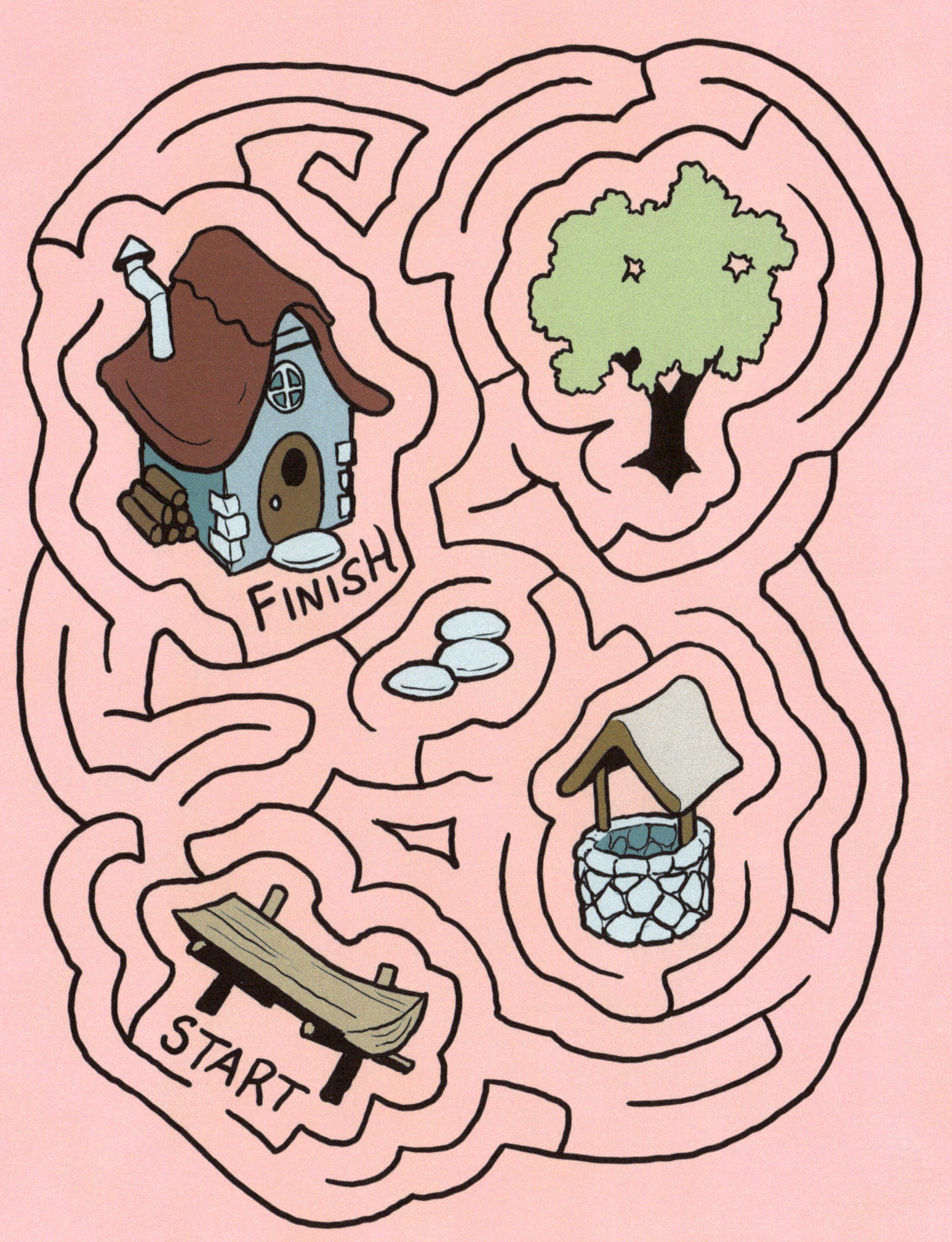

FINISH
START

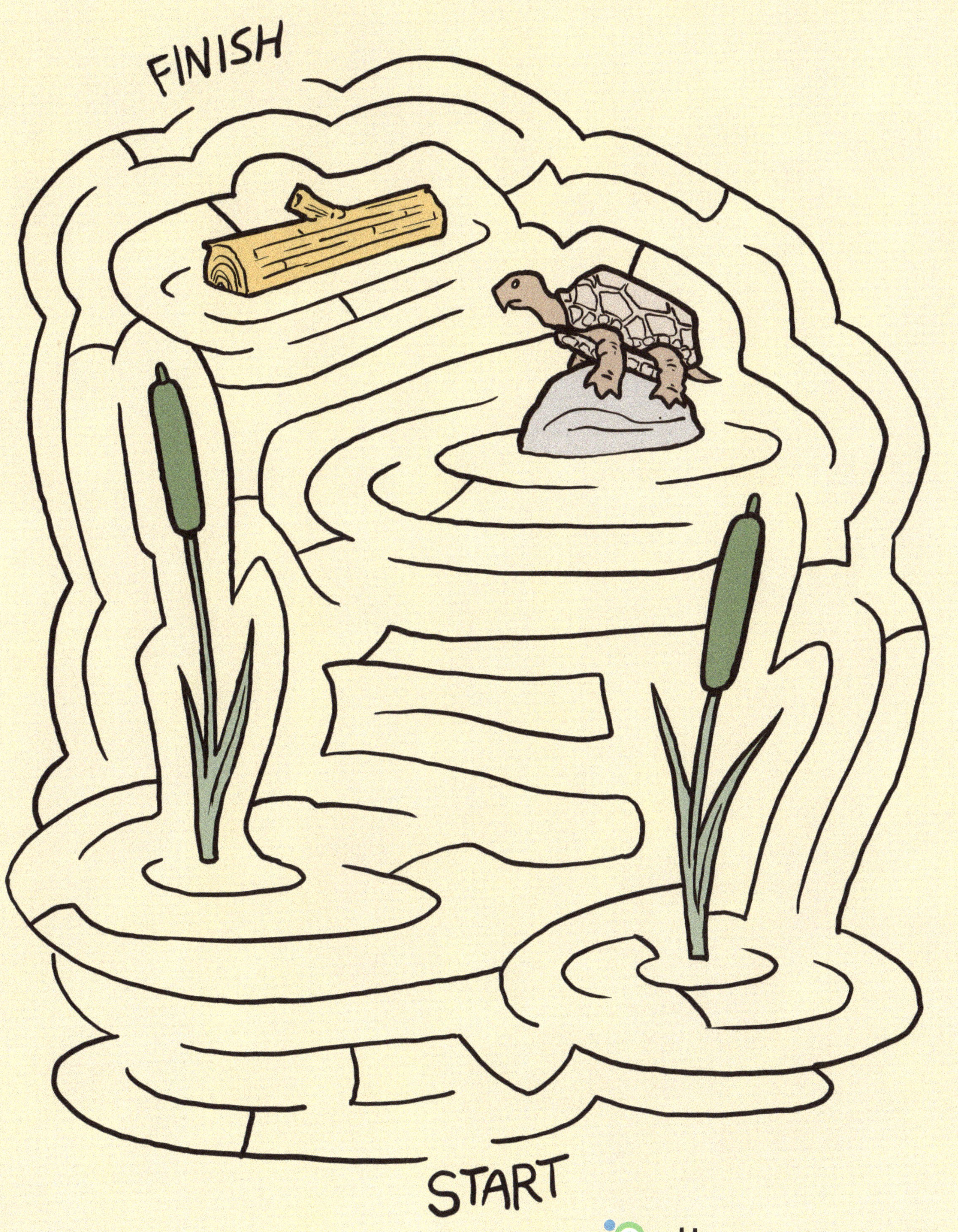

FINISH
START
THE Seltzer METHOD

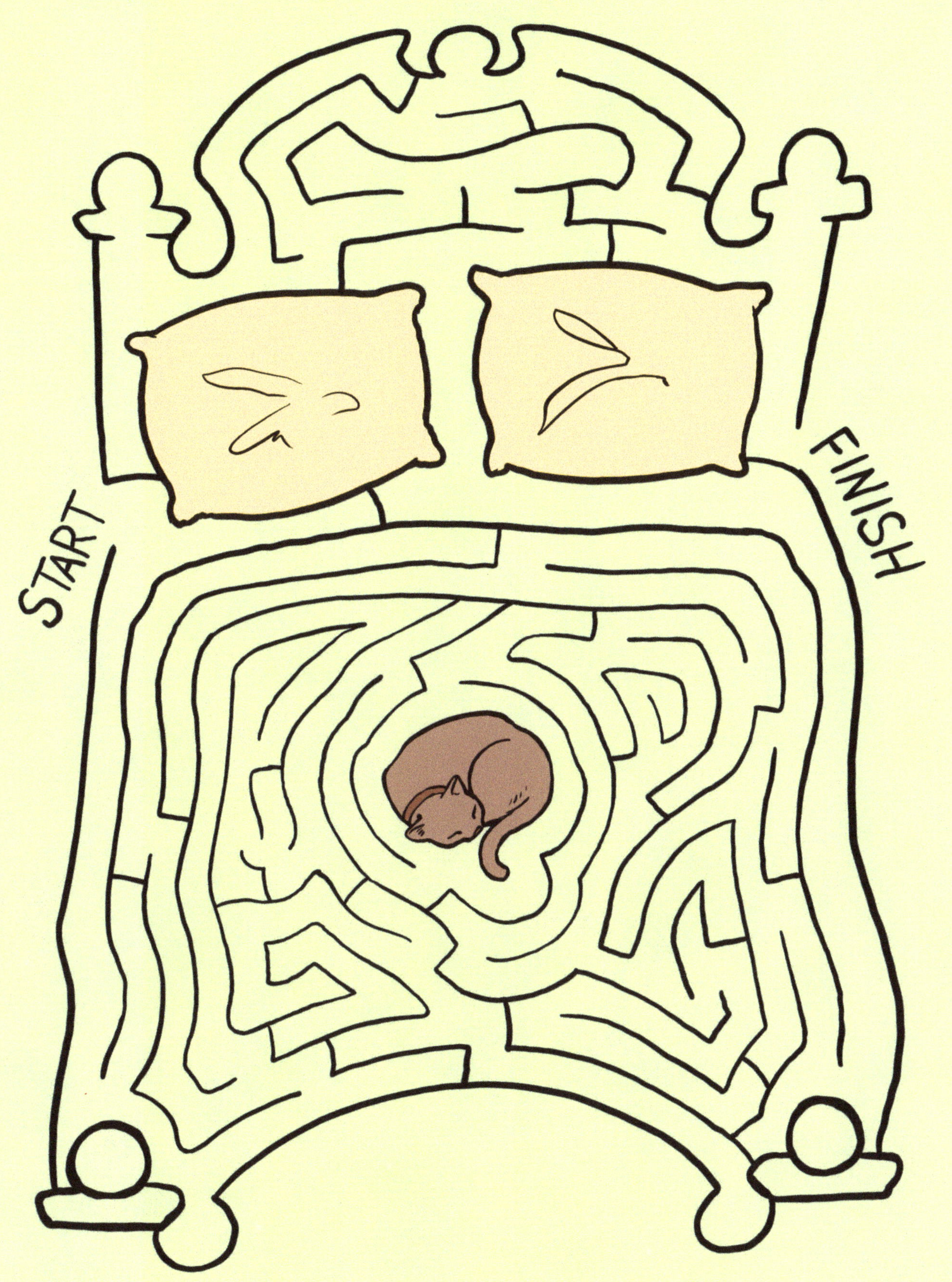

START
FINISH

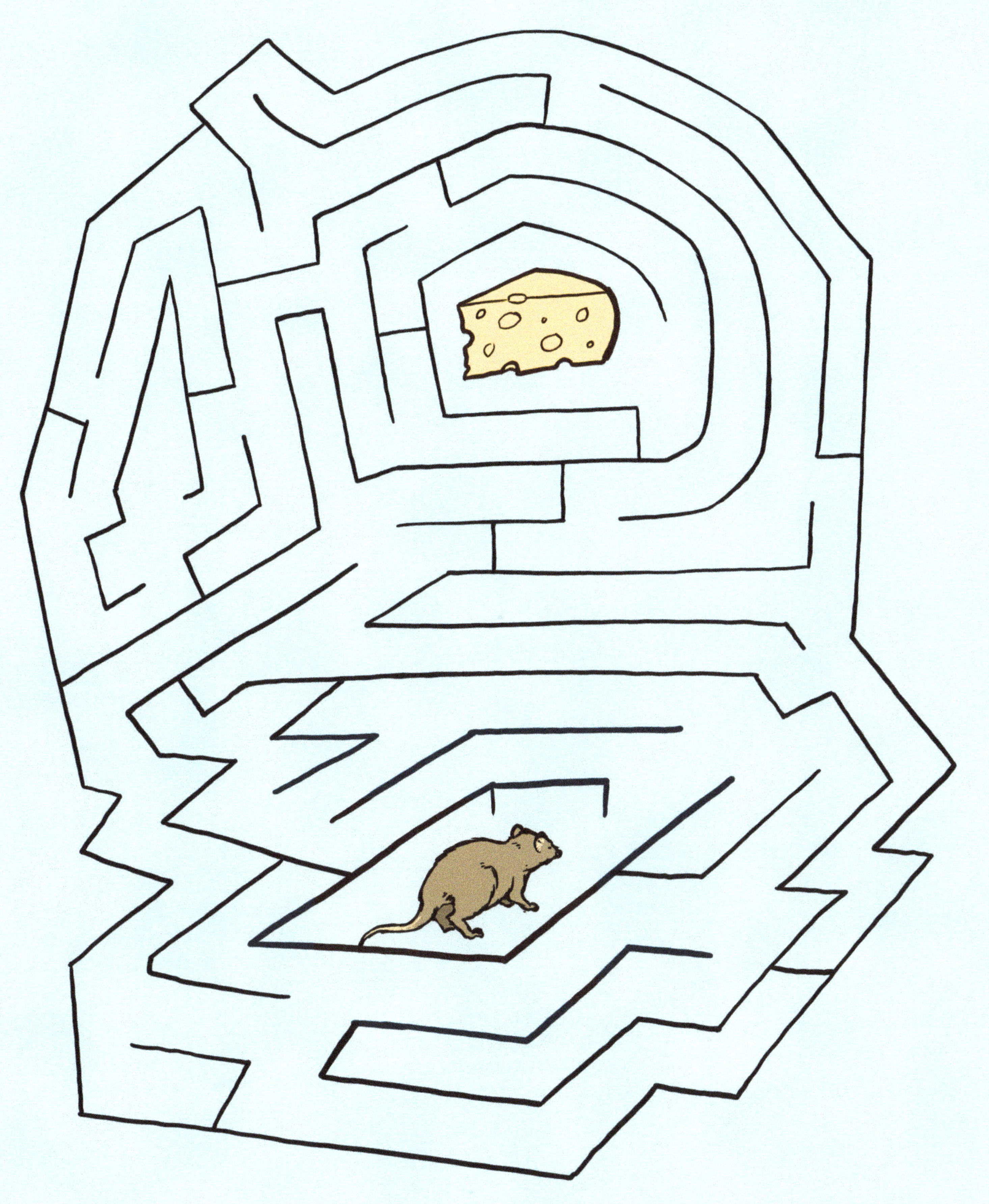

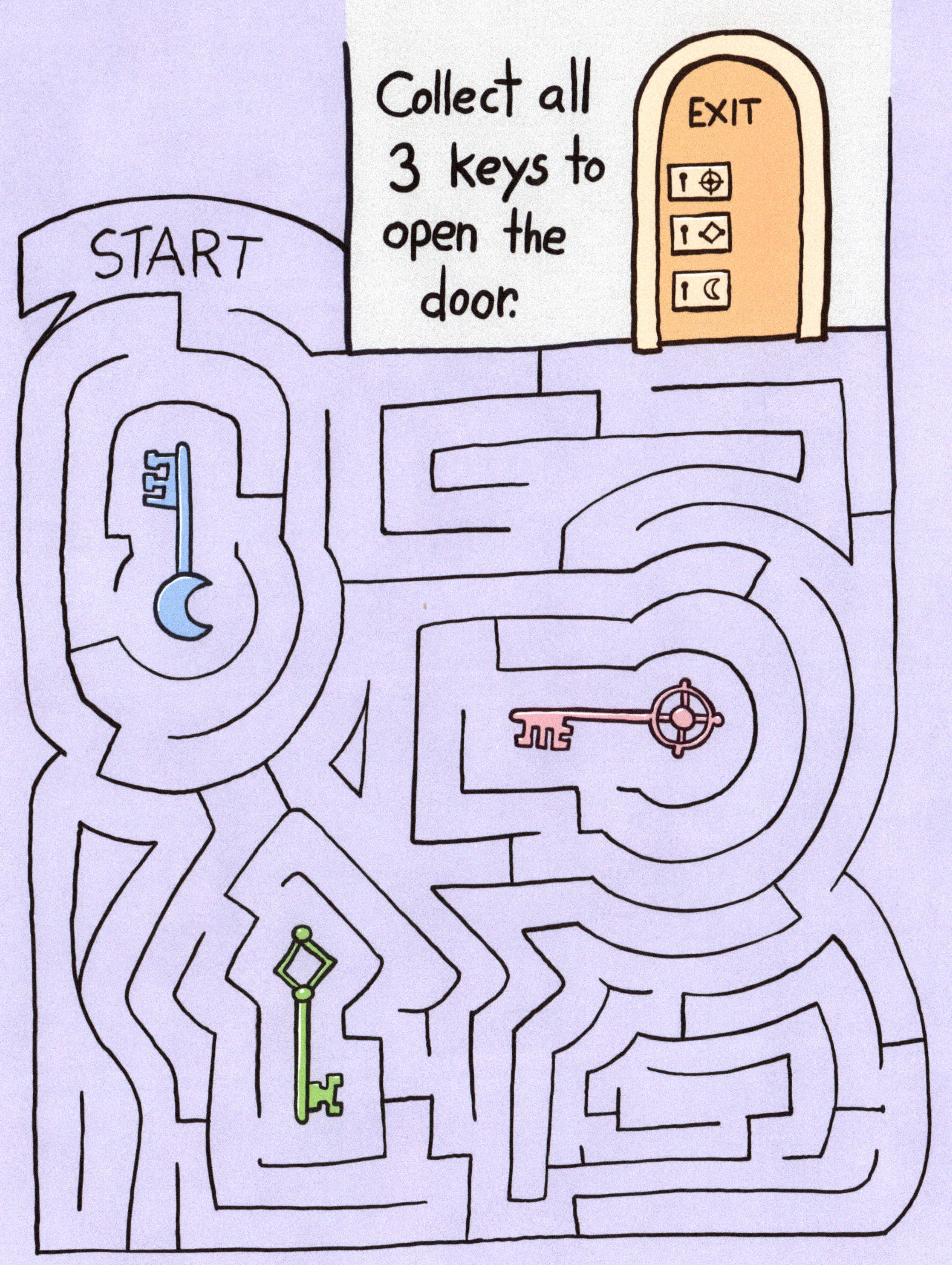

START
Collect all
3 keys to
open the
door.
EXIT
THE Seltzer METHOD

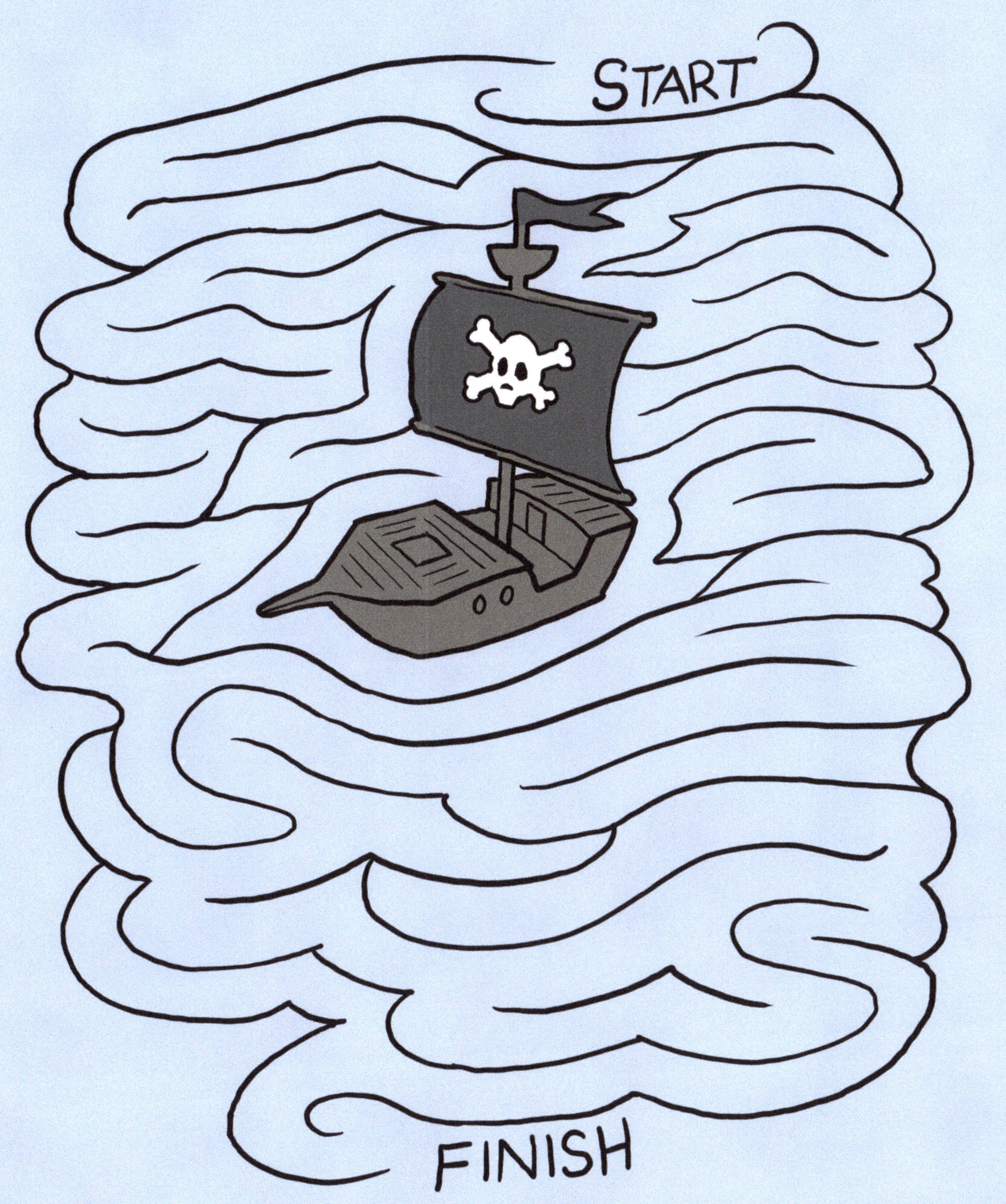

START
FINISH

**Making Mazes**  LESSONS, CHALLENGES, & WORKBOOK

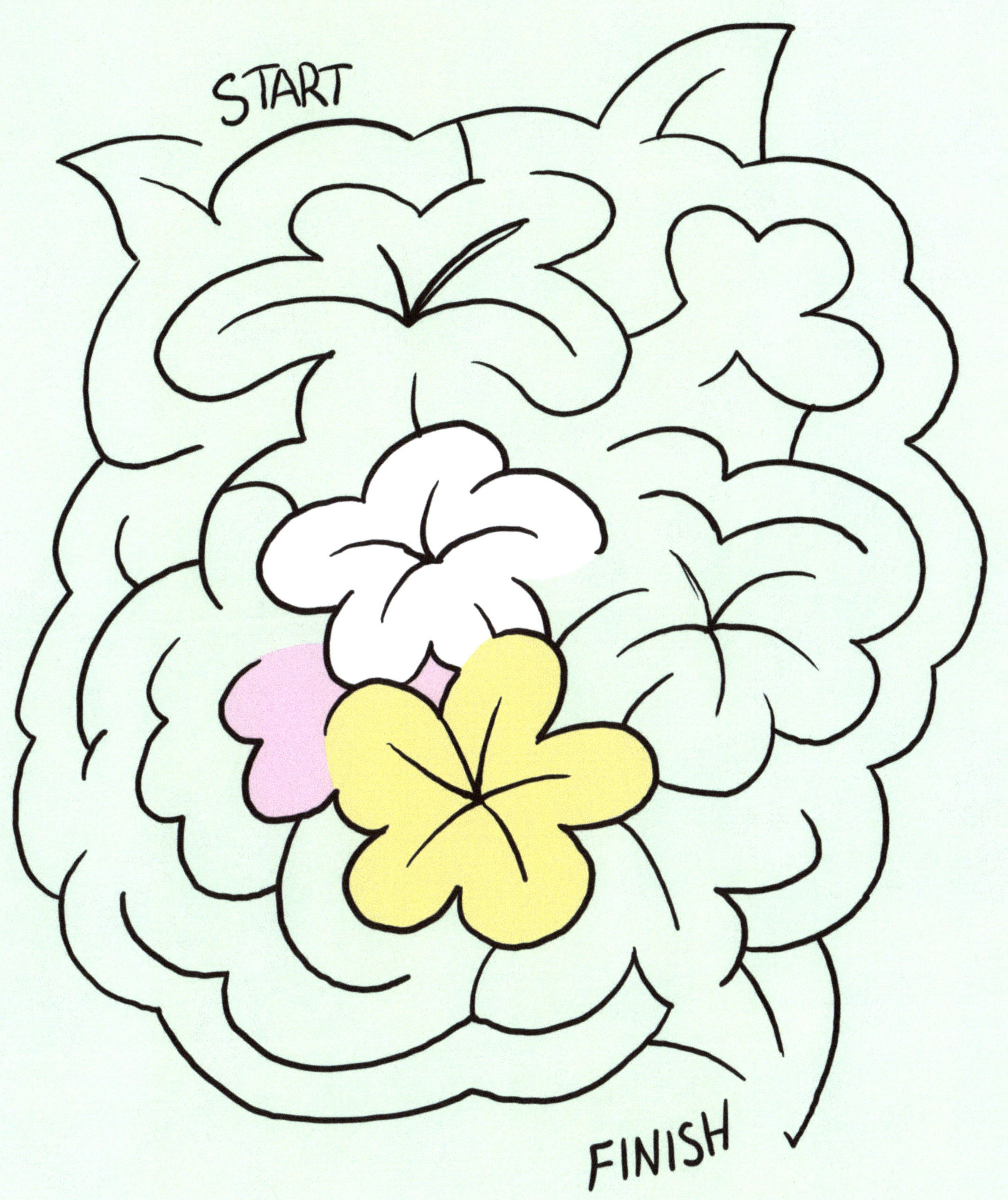

START
FINISH

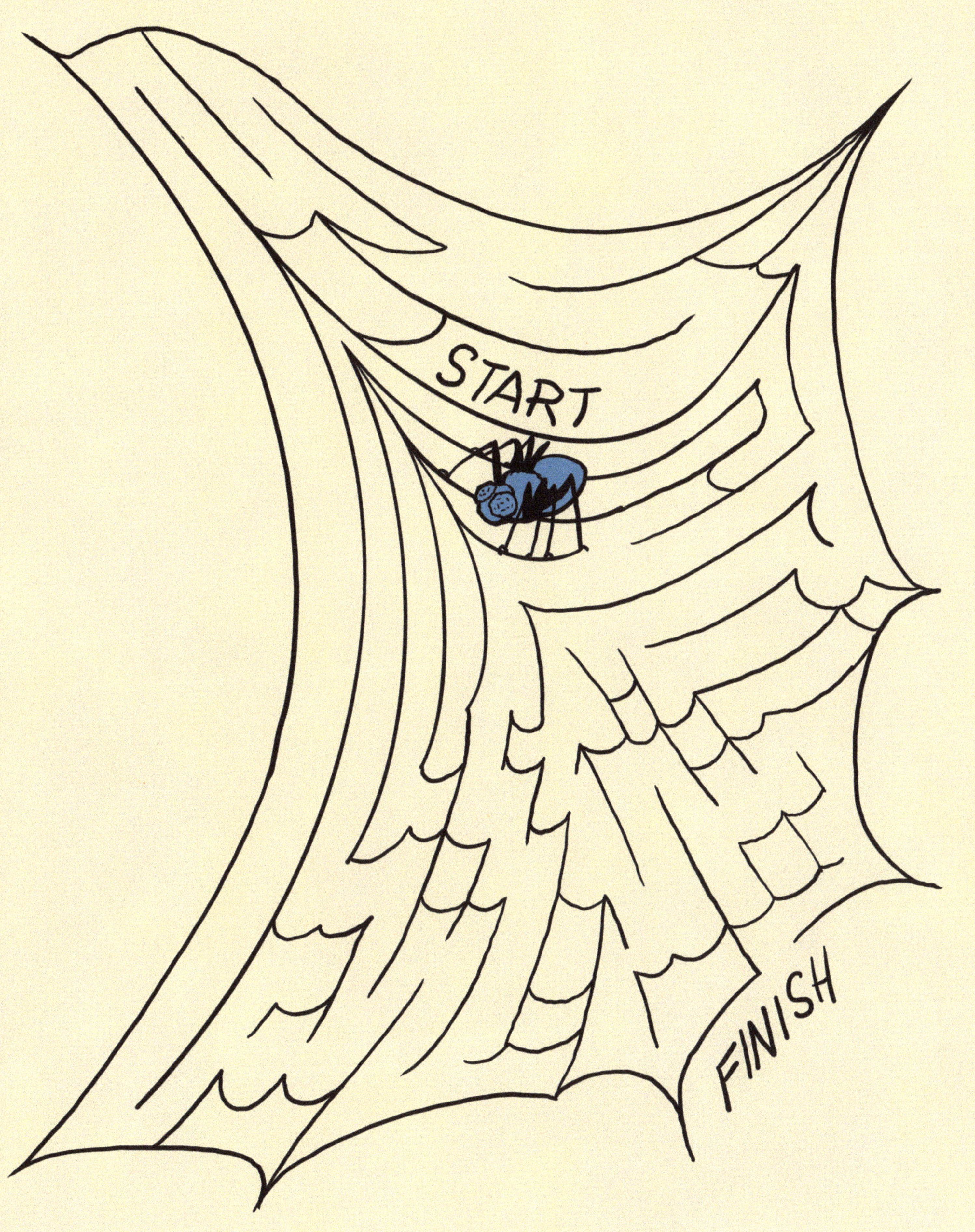



THE Seltzer METHOD

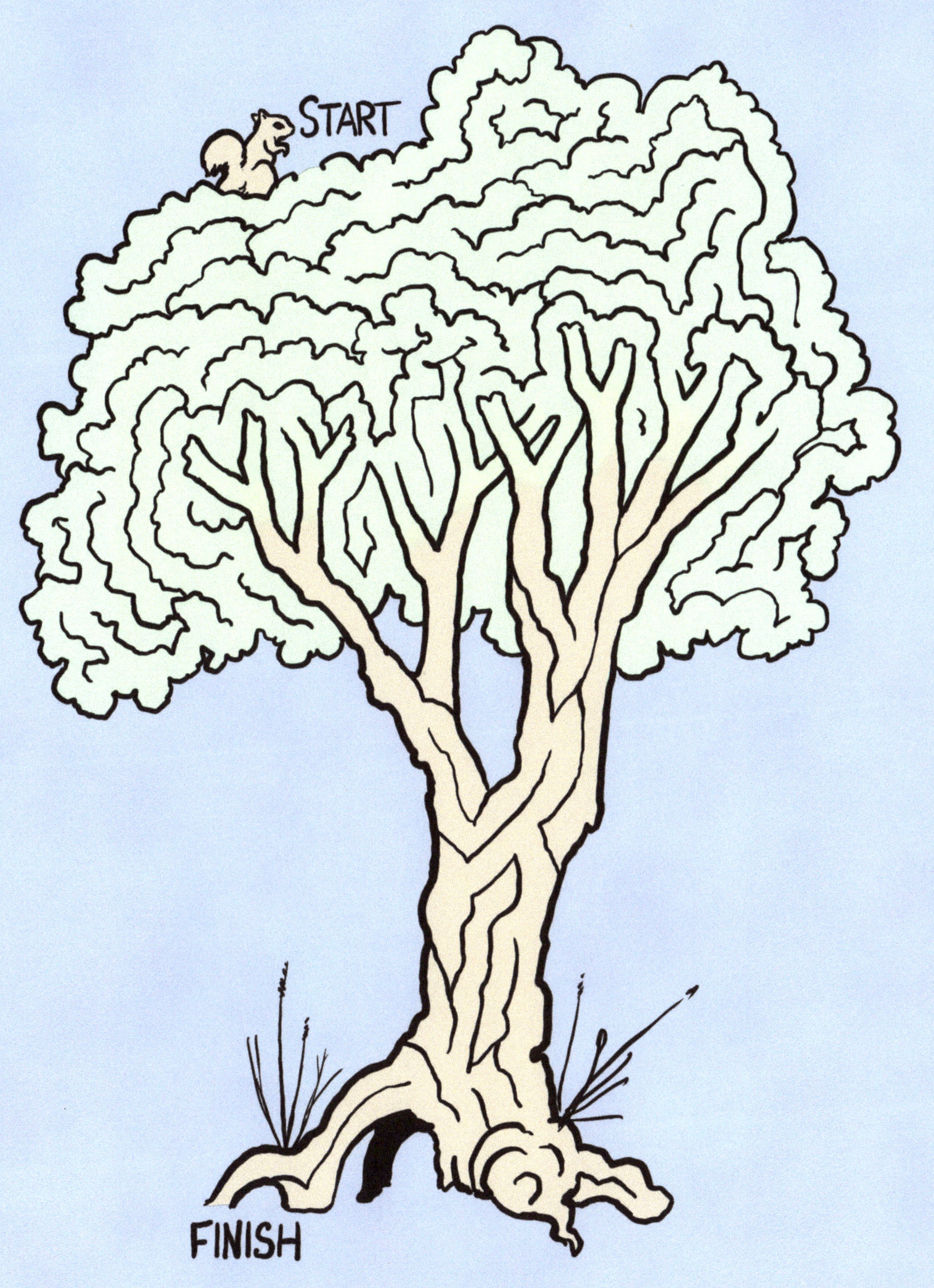

START
FINISH

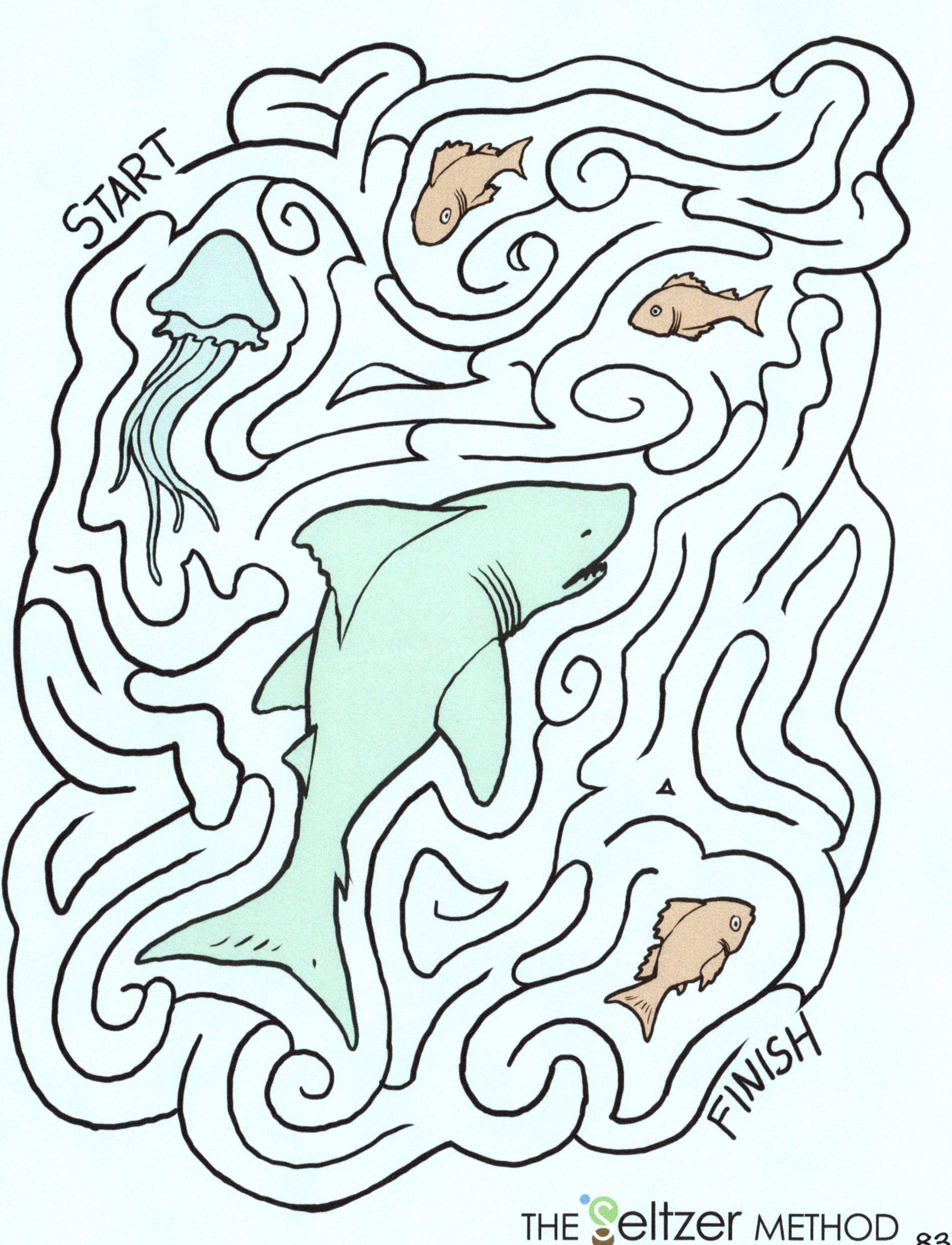

START
FINISH
THE Seltzer METHOD
83

**Making Mazes** LESSONS, CHALLENGES, & WORKBOOK

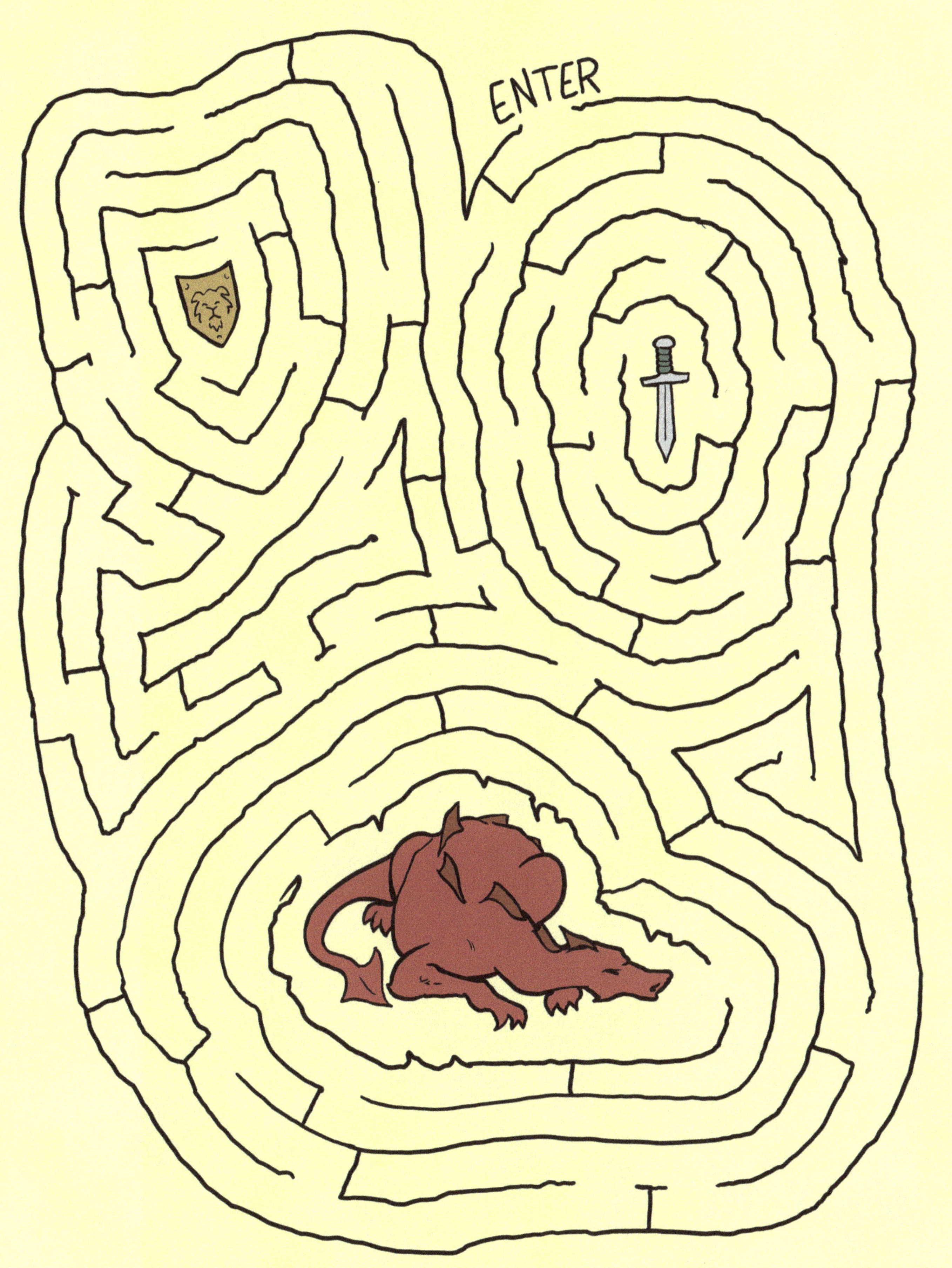
ENTER

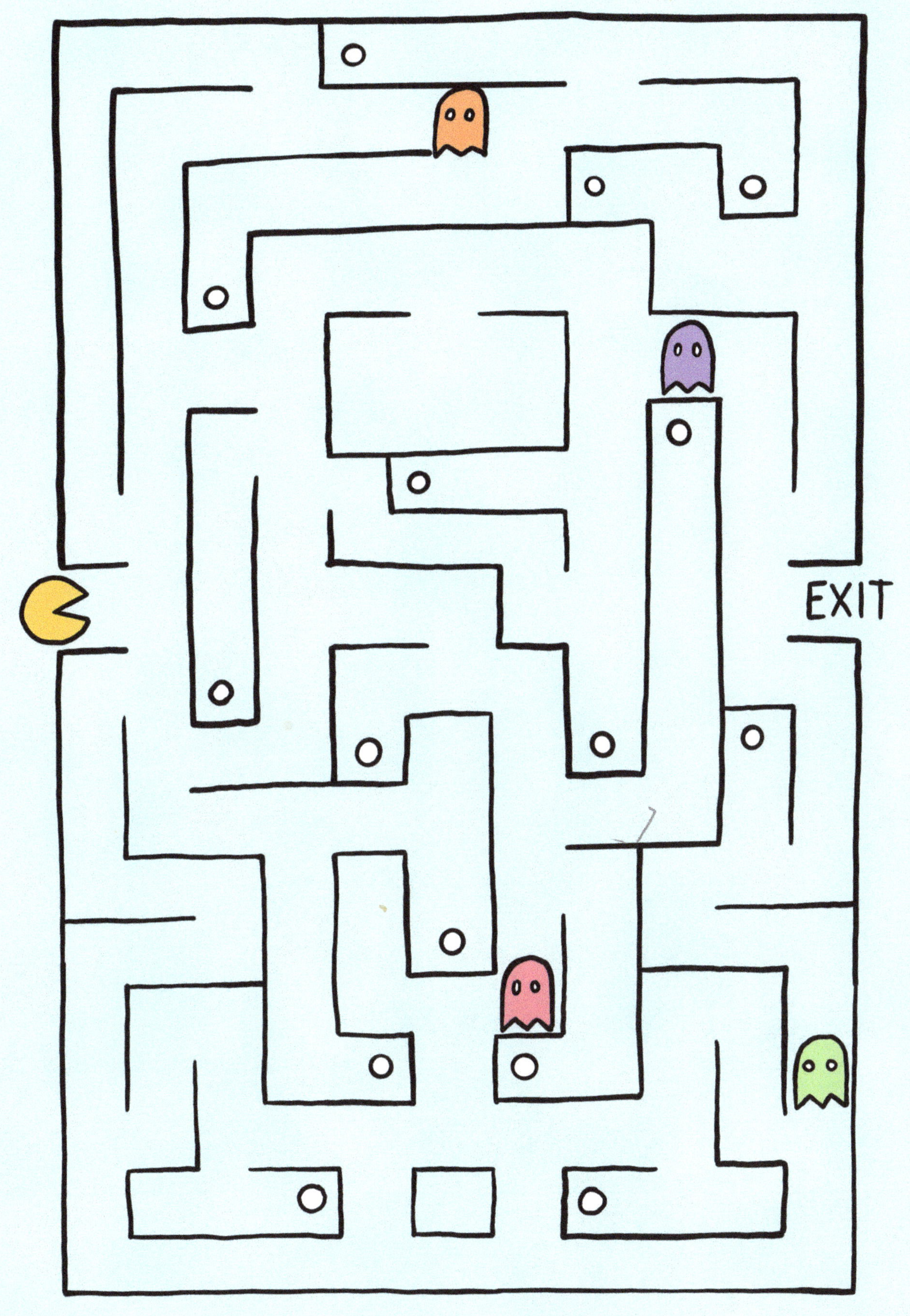

EXIT

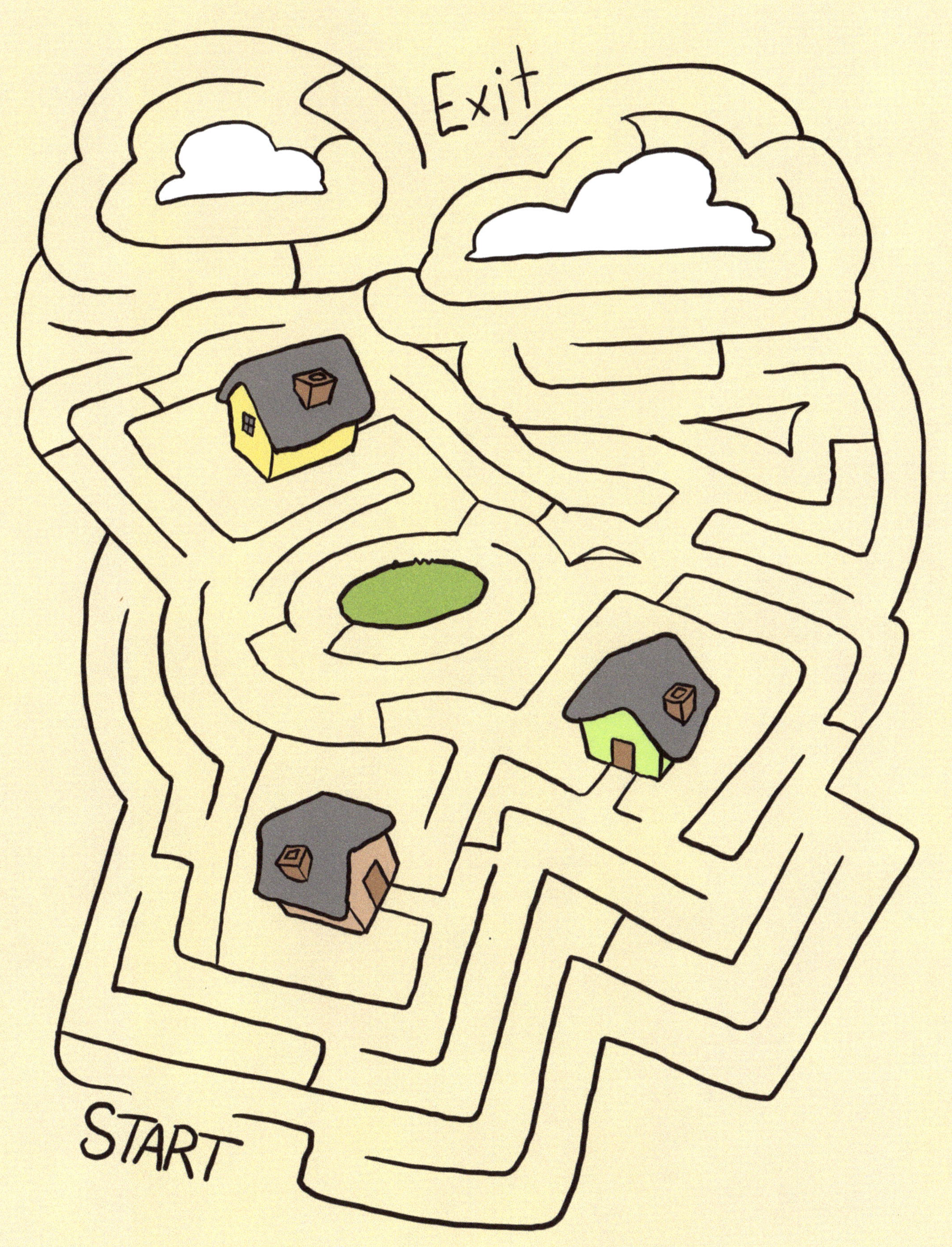

Exit
START

START
FINISH
THE Seltzer METHOD
91

**Jerry Joe Seltzer** is an artist and online teacher. His work has appeared in countless books, magazine, TV shows, movies, and products. You can watch videos and join Jerry's live classes at TheSeltzerMethod.com